*Coastline*UK

AMAZING VIEWS FROM THE AIR

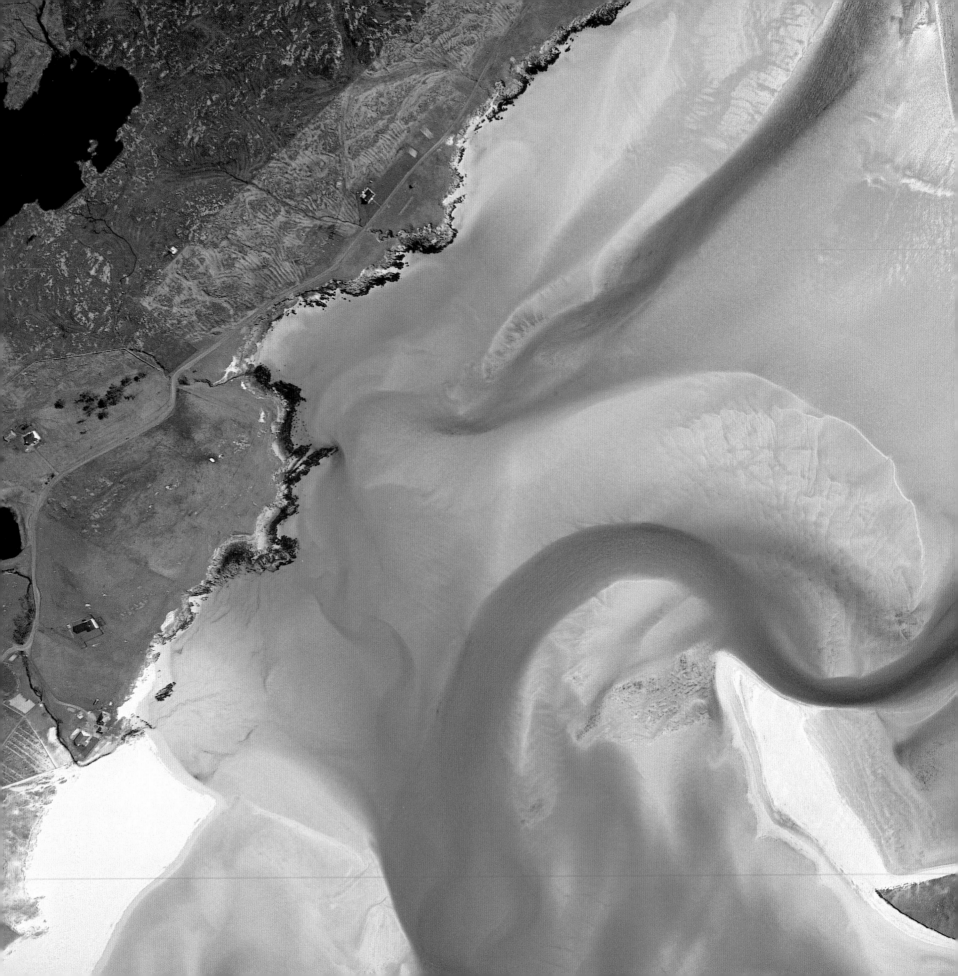

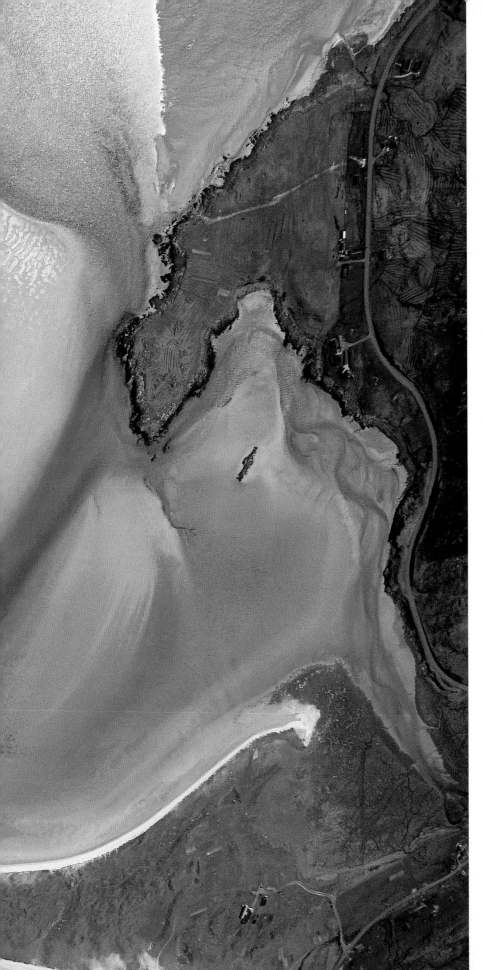

RICHARD COOKE

*Coastline*UK

AMAZING VIEWS FROM THE AIR

Thames & Hudson

St Ives, Cornwall

Blackpool, Lancashire

TITLE PAGES
Western Isles, Scotland

White sands, ancient rocks and
swirling currents make the Western
Isles the setting of some of the most
extraordinary combinations of form
and colour in the whole of Britain.

Western Isles, Scotland

The Humber Bridge, East Coast

coasts of northern ireland & scotland 100

eastcoast 168

For Gilly, James, Lucy and Charlie

Richard Cooke prepares to photograph
part of the coastline of the Western Isles.

As we flew over the coastline in the Outer Hebrides, I looked down at the swirl of turquoise sea and sand beneath the helicopter. With its vibrant, clear colours, it was difficult to believe that this was the British coast – it looked more like the sea off a coral island in the South Pacific. At that point I had already been flying around our coastline for a few weeks and had been constantly amazed and delighted by its variety and beauty. Even places that looked uninteresting from the ground could take on a strange and dramatic organic quality from above.

I had been commissioned by the Royal Mail to produce a set of ten stamps on the British coast. My brief was open: to gather images which would cover different areas and picture the diversity and beauty of the coastline. Although I was extremely flattered, I was also somewhat apprehensive about the enormity of the project. I wanted to shoot straight down from a helicopter in order to give my images a graphic edge. As a helicopter cannot hover on its side, it would have to fly a steep-banked turn over the area that I wanted to photograph. While the helicopter turns, the world seems to rise up and fill the doorway before spinning and descending again, which does not give you much time to frame and take the pictures!

The first helicopter trip I made on this project highlighted the difficulty of starting a job like this in the middle of winter. I flew from Norwich to the Norfolk coast in brilliant sunshine, only to find low cloud hugging the shore. I managed to take one picture and then had to call it a day. The next flight was in January. It was freezing on the ground but it was a beautiful, bright, clear sunny day. The cold, crisp air and the smattering of snow on the ground gave a strange blue quality to the shadows of the rocks below and, as I looked straight down at the coast, I knew that this experience was going to produce some very unusual, beautiful and diverse images.

As we flew westwards from Bristol along the Somerset coast, I began to see organic forms in the coastline far below: a spur of rock seemed to resemble a

ballerina's leg; the ribcage of a long, rotten, wooden barge sticking out of the sand looked like a giant pair of false eyelashes; vegetation took on the appearance of an ear; and mud and silt bulged with arteries and veins. My next stretch of coast – from Southend along Kent's shoreline – could not have been more different, with its abundance of man-made structures: houses overlooking the sea, groynes to protect the beaches, and footpaths and agriculture perilously close to the crumbling white cliffs.

I decided to go to Dorset where the coastguard had agreed to let me accompany the rescue team on a couple of training exercises. Their big Sikorsky 61N had no more difficulty banking right over than the small helicopters I had been using, and the highly skilled pilots and crew knew all the most beautiful and unusual bits of the coast. The underwater veins of Chesil Beach, echo-like ripples of Lulworth Cove and the Caribbean-like beach at Studland Bay all made a lasting impression on me.

Back in Southend we flew north up through Essex and Suffolk. The coast here is very flat and, from the ground, not particularly exciting. From the air it is a completely different story. There are large areas of exotic patterns – some of which look like cross sections of the brain, or an alien foetus – phallic sea defences and the graphic tidiness of Felixstowe docks.

Northern Ireland was next with its wonderful, varied coastline, stretching from the Giant's Causeway and the surf-dashed rocks and coves of the north to the gently rolling coast of County Down. Strangford Lough is a tidal seawater lough with hundreds of little islands. Most of them are farmed; some of the larger ones are arable and some smaller ones have only a dozen or so sheep. These islands are often amazing shapes and conjure up all sorts of images – a leaping dolphin, a stingray or even Mickey Mouse!

From Northern Ireland I flew straight to Scotland while the good weather held. Here the coast has a different character again. Bright green cliff-top golf courses and fields, razor-sharp rocky outcrops and areas of swirling sand. The sea was so calm and clear that I could not quite see where it met the shore, and the colours of the rocks were intensified by the water. On the west coast and the Isle of Bute the water was darker and more brackish but the colours were still amazing. The clouds were starting to build up and were reflecting on the still, calm surface of the sea.

After a couple of weeks processing and editing film, I journeyed to the Outer Hebrides, flying with the coastguard again. This was the most spectacular trip of all.

The place had everything: snow-white sands and blue sea in the shallows, white surf and jet-black sea by the rocks.

Another trip with the coastguard was based at Lee-on-the-Solent and coincided with the 'round the island' yacht race. This time the weather was really awful. We had several 'emergencies' involving yachts in the race, which turned out to be false alarms, and, disappointingly, I only got two shots of coastal erosion on the Isle of Wight.

Cornwall, my next destination, was as beautiful as I had expected. However, the tide was out and school holidays had not yet begun, which meant that I was unable to get the crowded beach and surfing pictures that I wanted. I felt I must include people having fun on the beach and decided to go back after the schools had broken up, at high tide when people would be less spread out on the beach. In late July the place still oozed its natural beauty but now there were also surfers and donkeys. The tide was in, people were sunbathing, bouncy castles were on the sand, the sun was shining and all was right with the world.

There were two more areas I still wanted to photograph to get a thoroughly representative view of the British coast: Yorkshire and Blackpool. I hired a helicopter from Humberside and flew to Whitby and then followed the coast down from there. Clean, calm waters enabled me to see through the shallows to the colour-enhanced rocks below. Further south towards Flamborough Head, these rocks looked like coral under the water. Suddenly the sea fog came in with amazing speed and the whole coast disappeared under a thick white blanket. We flew back as quickly as possible and drove to pick up another helicopter on the other side of the country to take a look at Blackpool. This was a visual culture shock. It was a riot of colour on the piers, with water slides, bungee jumps, roller coasters and all the fun of the fair. From above the pleasure beach looked like a piece of modern art or the top of a pinball machine.

It was such a great privilege to fly over so much of the coast. The images have been a pleasant surprise to many people who tend to think of our own coast as drab and cold. With over 7,000 miles of shoreline, however, Britain has not only one of the longest but also one of the most beautiful and diverse coastlines in Europe.

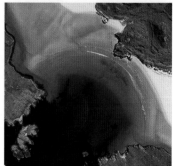

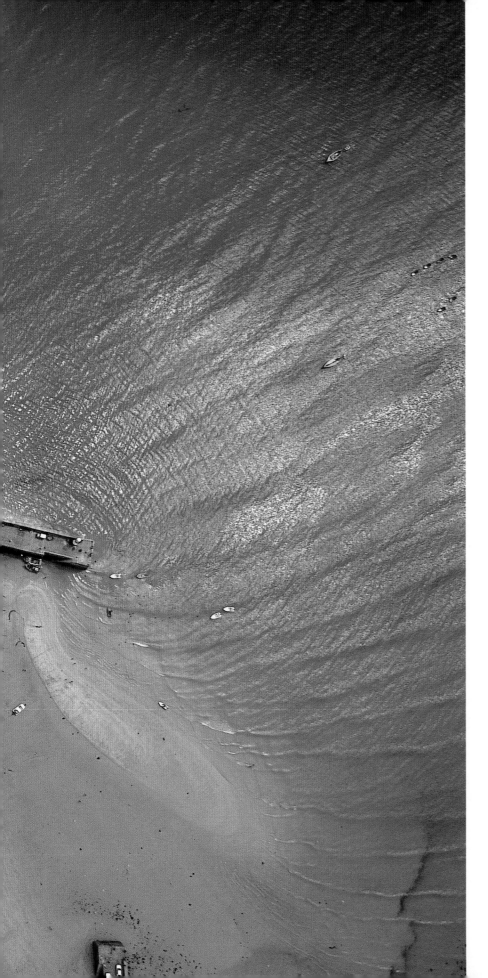

From Kent to Devon and Cornwall, the south coast of Britain announces the variety which characterizes the whole coastline of the United Kingdom. The White Cliffs of Dover, symbolic of national identity, take on unexpected forms under this unique aerial scrutiny, while the holiday resorts and sheltered harbours which front the Channel look touchingly vulnerable from the air. And finally, there is the granite promontory of Cornwall to take the full force of the Atlantic.

St Ives, Cornwall
Often described as a 'jewel', St Ives is a thriving town at the south-western tip of Cornwall, just around the corner from Lands End. As in past centuries, life in the town centres around the harbour, where fishing boats still moor alongside granite piers, and many pleasure craft find a safe haven.

Broadstairs and the Isle of Thanet, Kent
Although it looks like it was built in medieval times to resist the invading armies of foreign foes, Neptune's Tower was actually created by Lord Holland in the mid-eighteenth century as part of his vast folly, Kingsgate Castle. Standing proud on the cliffs between White Ness and Foreness Point, the tower was constructed in a style which reflects the plan of Deal Castle just a few miles south. In more recent times it finally fulfilled its defensive role when it was used as an observation post during World War II.

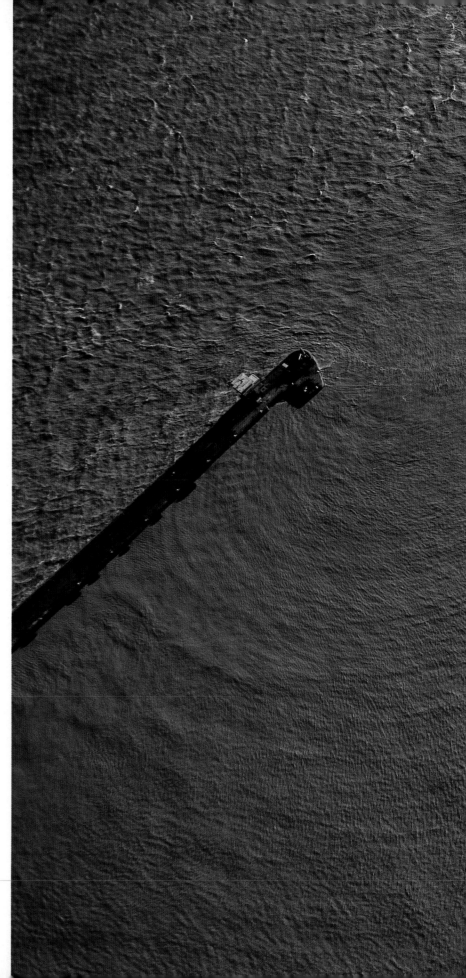

Dover Harbour, Kent

Dover has long been one of Britain's most important maritime settlements. Almost 2,000 years ago the Romans recognized its importance and established a naval base, Classis Britannica, here. In the Middle Ages Dover became a Cinque Port, an alliance of five ports in Kent and Sussex, sanctioned by Edward the Confessor to provide coastal defence. One of the most powerful castles in the country was built here to guard the harbour and defend the realm. Situated, as it is, at the narrowest point in the English Channel, Henry VIII also realized the strategic importance of Dover and enlarged the port to accommodate many ships from his newly formed Royal Navy. Today Dover has become known as the 'Gateway to Britain' and is one of the busiest ferry ports in Europe.

Kent Coast

Britain's coastline has always been vital to the economics of the country and has been subject to a wide range of uses as a result. The popularity of living on the coast, industrial disturbance and environmental changes all contribute to coastal change, not all of which is to its benefit.

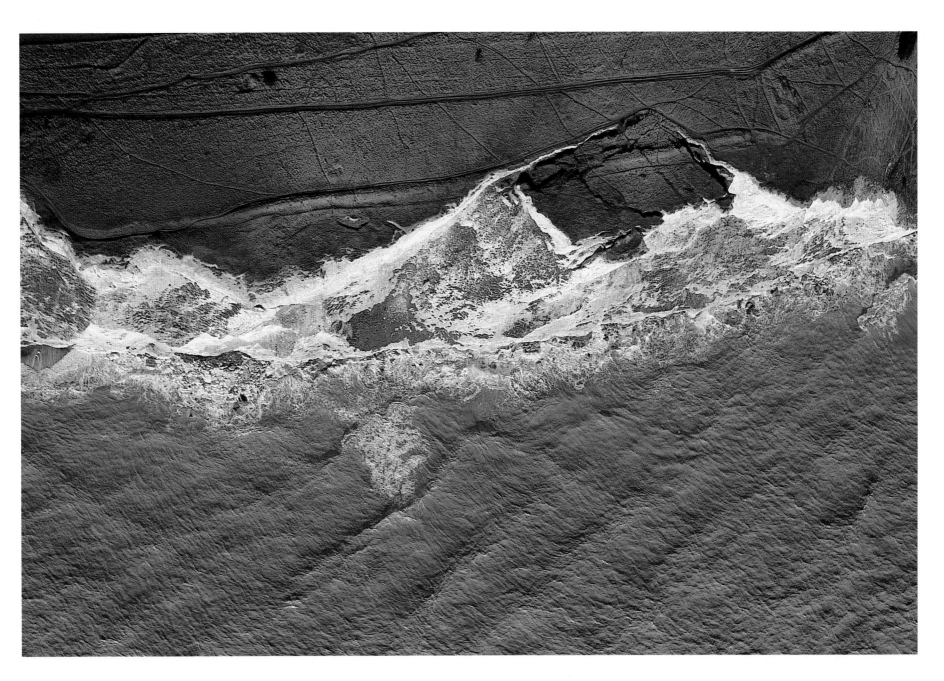

The White Cliffs of Dover, Kent

The White Cliffs of Dover are one of the best-known icons of the British coastline. The chalk that gives them their characteristic white appearance is made up of the skeletons of millions of tiny sea creatures, which settled on the seabed over one hundred and fifty million years ago.

The Romans built a *pharos*, or lighthouse, high up on the cliffs above Dover Harbour, to guide ships away from treacherous sand banks, now know as the Goodwin Sands, and into the safety of port. The flint remains of this very early navigational aid can still be seen close to Dover Castle and, at nearly 13 metres high, are the tallest Roman remains in Britain.

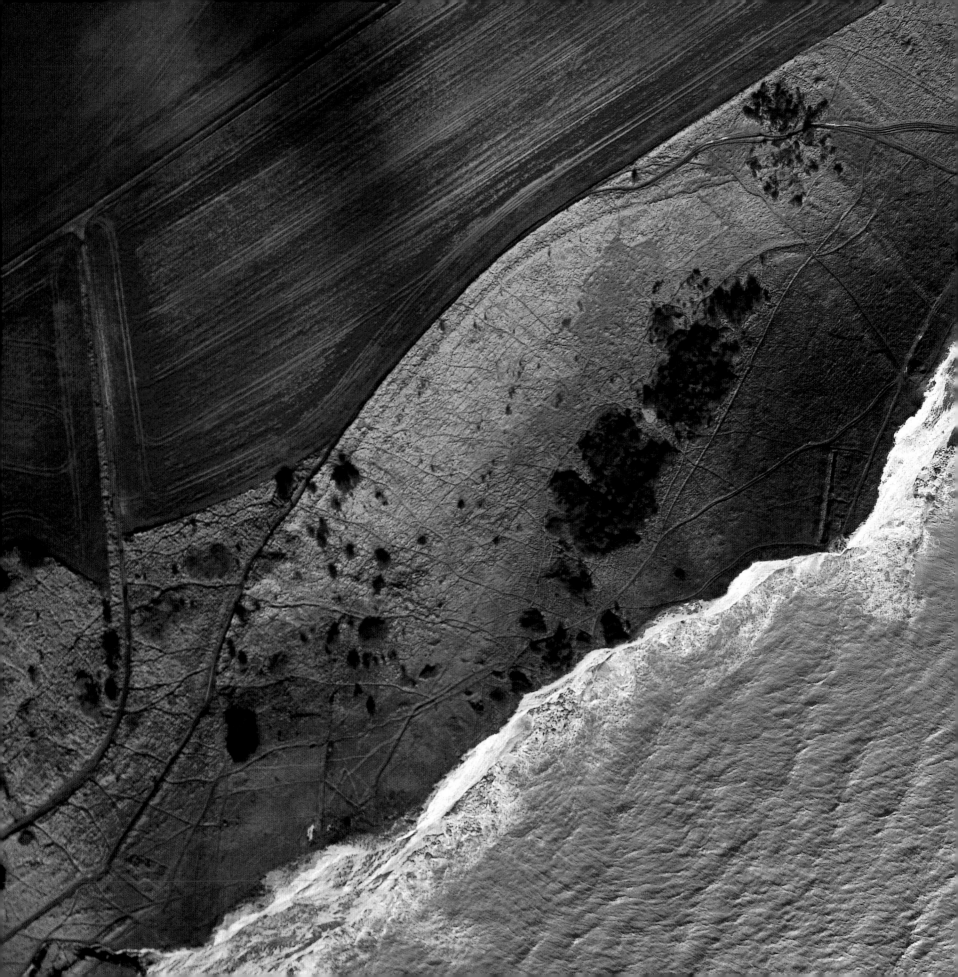

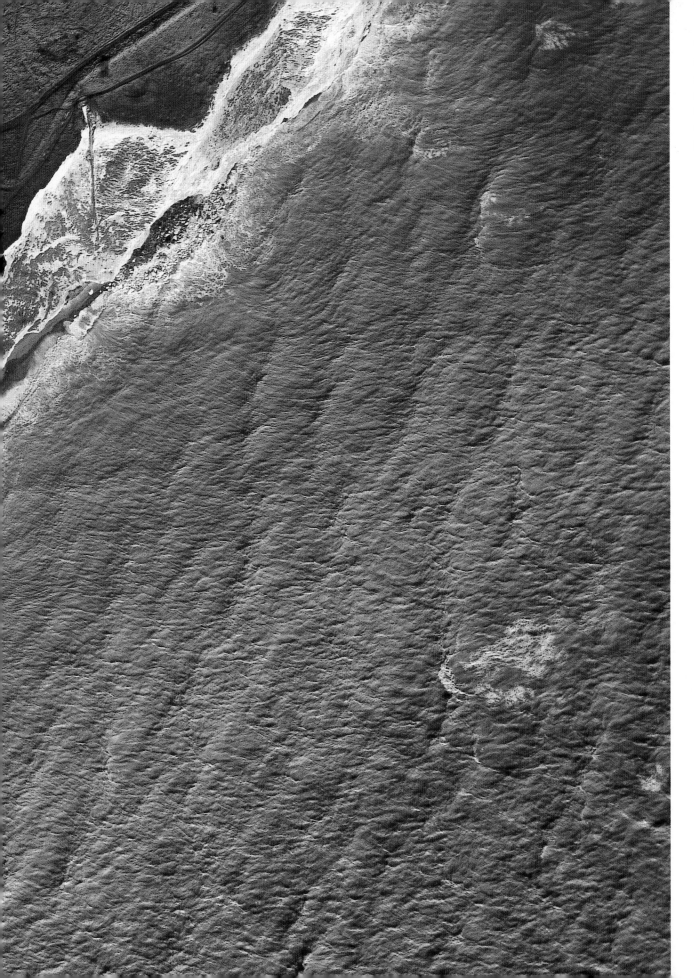

The White Cliffs of Dover, Kent
For many thousands of people every year, these world-famous cliffs are their first sighting of British soil. Few of these admirers realize, however, that the chalk is only kept white through a continual process of erosion by wind, rain and sea, which has been going on for millions of years.

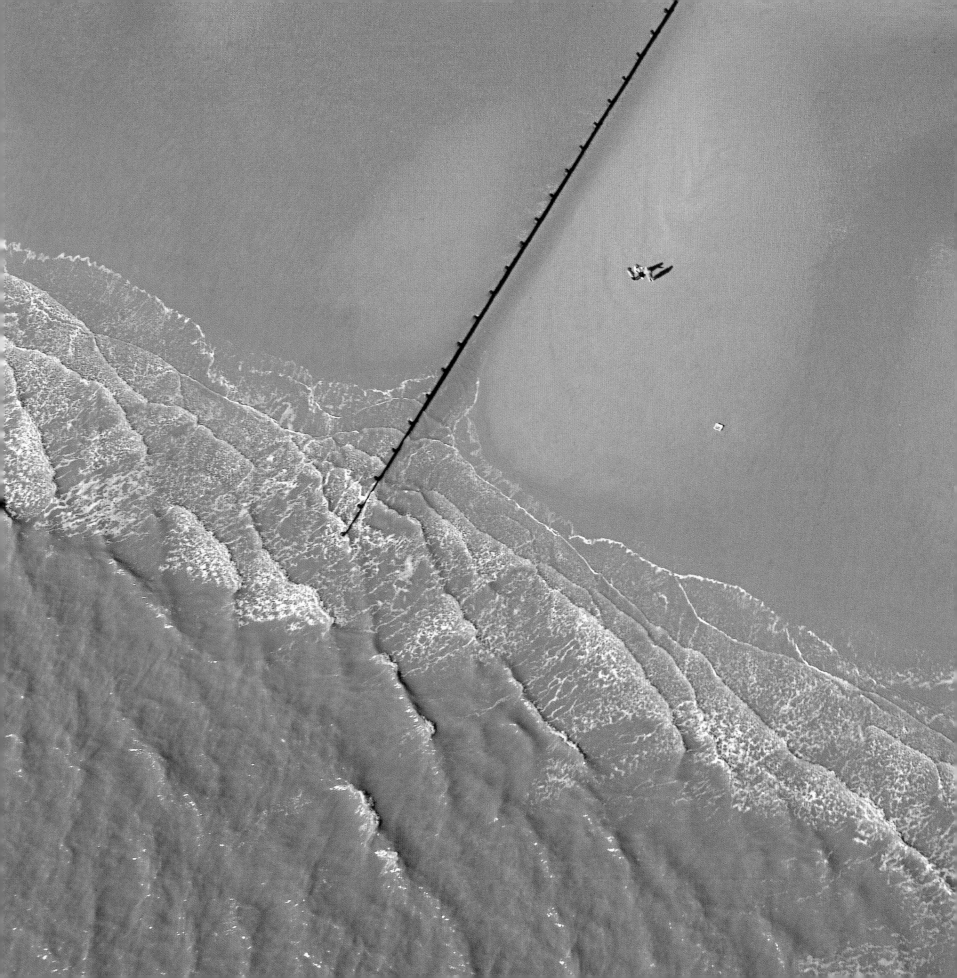

Kent Coast

Building castles and digging ditches in the sand has long been a popular pastime with holidaymakers at the beach. But few who enjoy the hundreds of miles of sandy beaches around our islands, like this one on the south Kent coast near Dymchurch, will realize how they came into being. The millions of tiny grains of sand are the result of centuries of weather erosion on sandstone and other soft rocks which make up the coastline. Endlessly changing at the whim of tide and wind, they are home to a surprisingly wide range of plants and animals.

Dorset Coast

In 2001 the spectacular Dorset coast became England's first area of natural heritage to receive World Heritage Site status. This recognizes the unique importance of this stretch of coastline for its archaeology and striking beauty. Nicknamed 'the Jurassic coast', it provides a 'walk in time through 180 million years in just 80 miles'.

Clavell Tower, Dorset

For almost 200 years, Clavell Tower has stood as the focal point above Kimmeridge Bay in Dorset. It was built in 1830 by Reverend John Richards Clavell as a folly and was also used as an observatory. The tower became a favourite getaway for Thomas Hardy and appeared on the frontispiece of his *Wessex Poems*. After World War I it was turned into a coastguard lookout. Fire destroyed the interior in the 1930s and it is now only a shell.

Isle of Wight

The Isle of Wight is one of the gems of the south coast of England. At 23 miles long and 13 miles wide, it offers a rich variety of coastal scenery: isolated bays; narrow ravines, known locally as 'chines'; a magnificent natural harbour at Newtown; and the precipitous chalk cliffs at the south-west end of the Island. Some of the beaches, particularly at Alum Bay, are famous for their coloured sands, running from deep red to greens and blues.

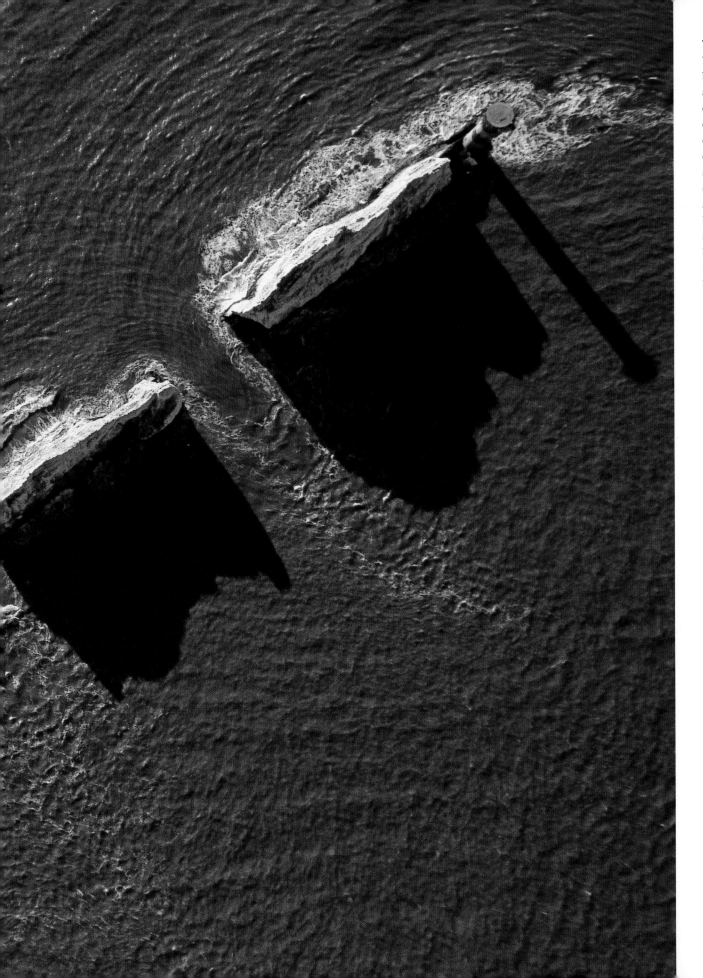

The Needles, Isle of Wight

These three 30-metre pinnacles of chalk, so well known to mariners entering the western Solent, are a remnant of a ridge that once joined the Isle of Wight to the mainland. Still eroding, there was once a fourth stack, known as 'Lott's Wife', which collapsed into the sea in 1764. On the cliffs overlooking the Needles stands Old Needles Battery, a Palmerston Fort hastily constructed in 1862 as a defence against the threatened French invasion. Although it saw little active service at that time, the battery was later to be the site of the world's first anti-aircraft gun, set up in 1913. In 1956 the headland became the engine-testing site for the Black Knight rocket, which was subsequently launched at Woomera in Australia.

NEXT PAGES
Studland Bay, Dorset

Probably one of the most popular beaches on the south coast of England, this beach is backed by a stretch of rare maritime heathland. It is said to be the only remaining heath where you can find all the indigenous British reptiles.

Over a million visitors each year enjoy the safe, sandy beaches of Studland, but for how much longer? Each year the sea is claiming back a metre of dunes, showing how the UK coast is perpetually changing in response to sea level and land movement – so rapid is the change at Studland that the beach huts have been moved twice in the last twenty-five years!

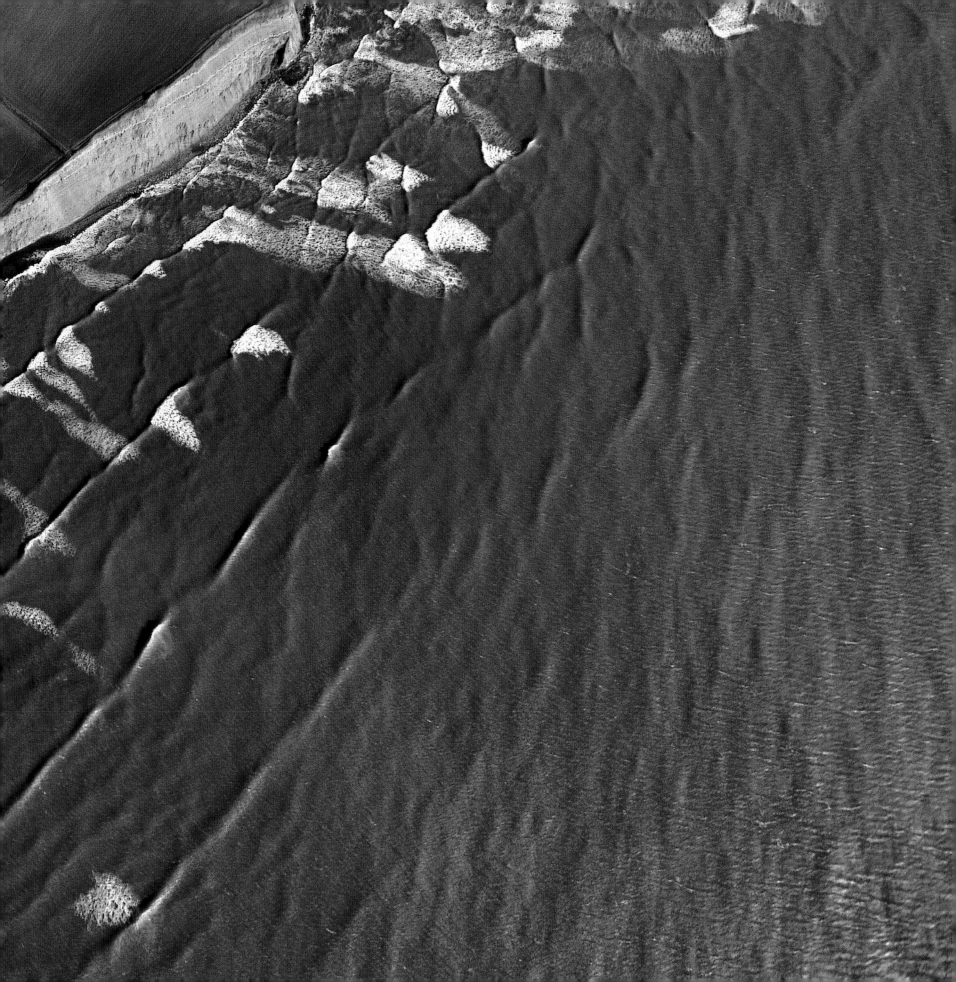

Dorset Coast

The Dorset coast can offer every kind of coastal landscape, from the rare chalkland pasture of the Isle of Purbeck, to deep golden-coloured cliffs at Golden Cap, plus a fossil-rich shoreline. All are hugely popular with summer visitors, particularly walkers.

Old Harry Rocks, Dorset

Looking like a piece from a giant jigsaw puzzle, the chalk cliffs of Dorset's Purbeck coast are amongst the most breathtaking in Britain. The chalk stacks, which mark the western side of the entrance to Poole Harbour, have the names 'the Spire', 'Old Harry' and 'Old Harry's Wife'. 'Old Harry' is one of the many British nicknames for the Devil and legend has it that he lay down for a nap on the top of these cliffs, leaving the shape of his hind leg in the chalk.

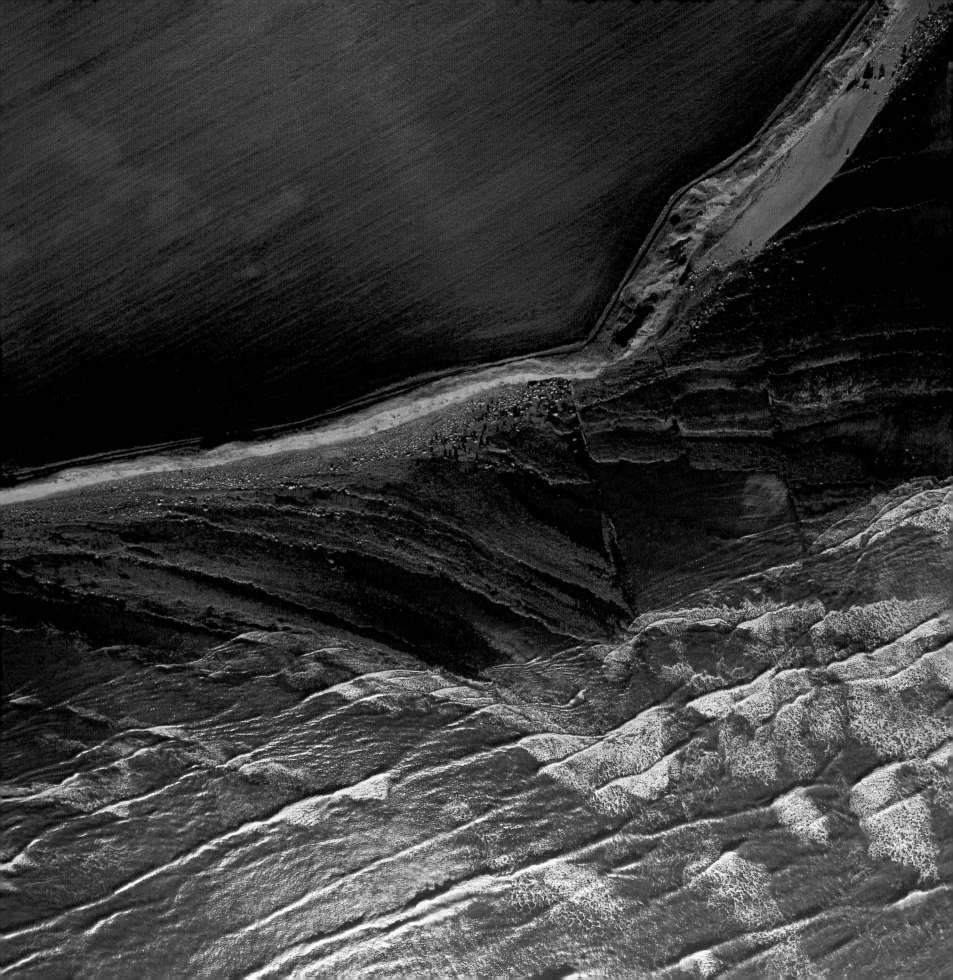

Dorset Coast

The Dorset coast is the best place in the world to see a complete sequence of rocks from the Triassic, Jurassic and Cretaceous periods. Across the length of Dorset, the rocks dip gently to the east, with the oldest rocks in the west dipping down below the sea to the east, allowing progressively younger rocks to form the cliffs.

NEXT PAGES
Durdle Door, Dorset

Looking like the face of a huge hammerhead shark, this magnificent natural rock arch carved by the sea is formed of the same Portland stone that was used to build St Paul's Cathedral in London. The first record of the name appears in 1811, when it was called Dirdale Door, which appears to be a corruption of a far older name perhaps meaning 'the hill with a hole'.

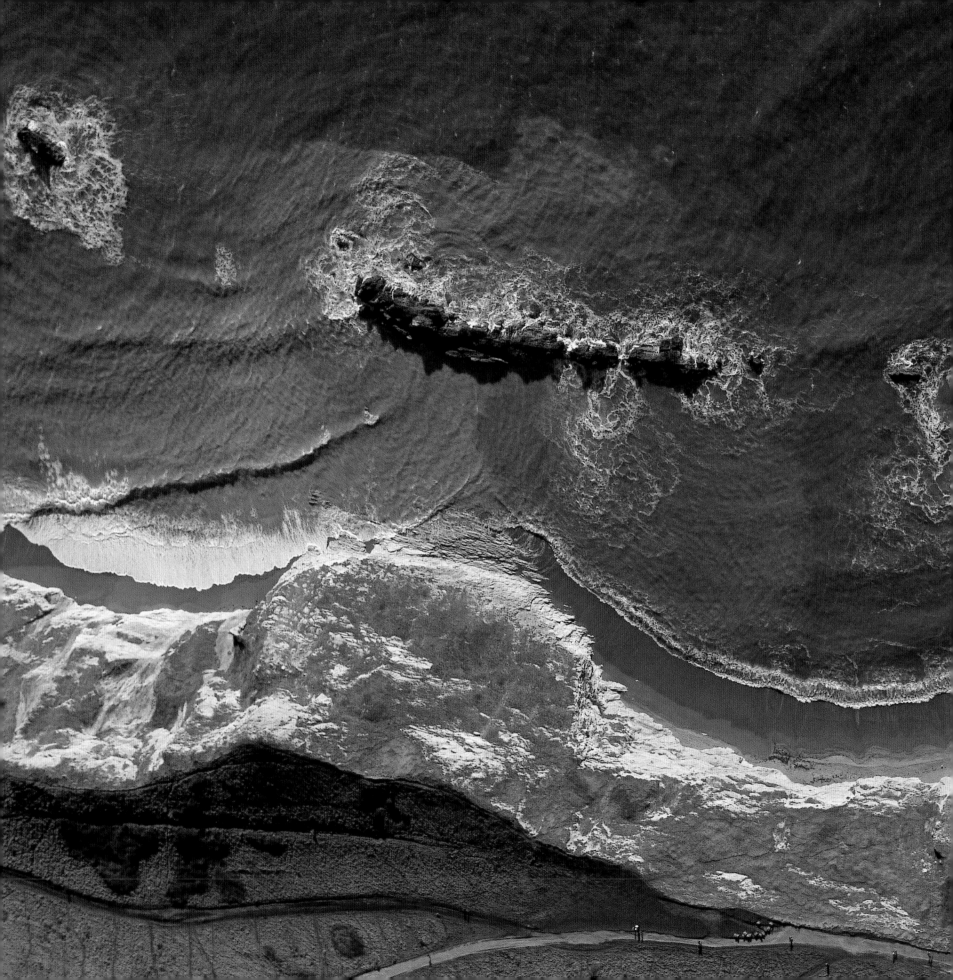

Weymouth Harbour, Dorset

It was here that sea bathing got its first royal seal of approval when King George III visited the town in 1789 and decided to take a dip. To the strains of the town band playing *God Save the King*, the King emerged from a bathing machine and took the plunge in front of an admiring crowd. As a result, wealthy Georgians followed suit and made visits to the seaside fashionable. Today a legacy of elegant Georgian buildings mingle with those of a busy port serving cross-channel ferries.

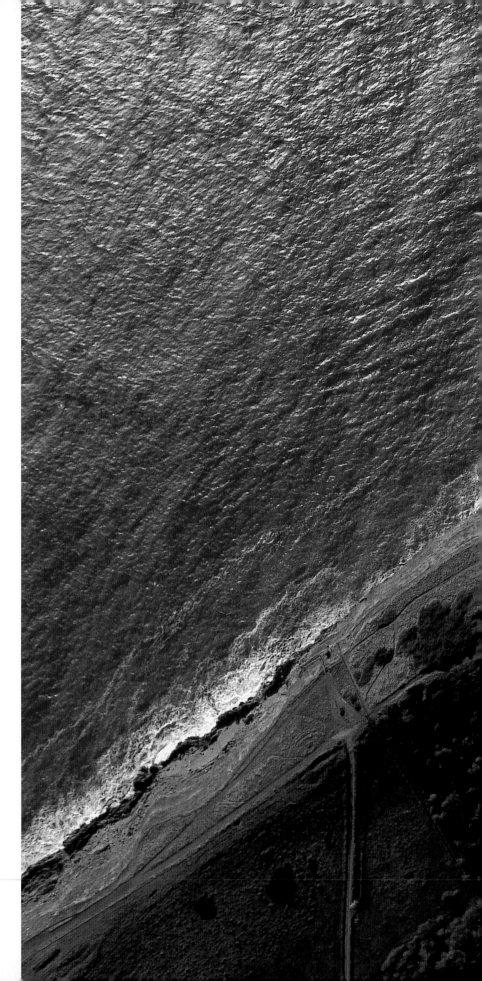

Lulworth Cove, Dorset

Lulworth Cove is a classic example of how the sea can nibble away at the shoreline until it creates a perfect scallop-shaped bay. The cove was formed by wave action which eroded the soft chalky rocks that lie behind a band of harder Portland limestone across the bay mouth and washed them away.

In the cliffs above the east side of the bay there is a fossil forest, which was created about one hundred and forty million years ago on land near a salty lagoon. Most of the fossils are empty moulds, but there are some pieces of fossilized tree to be seen, all showing the sort of ancient environment in which late Jurassic dinosaurs lived.

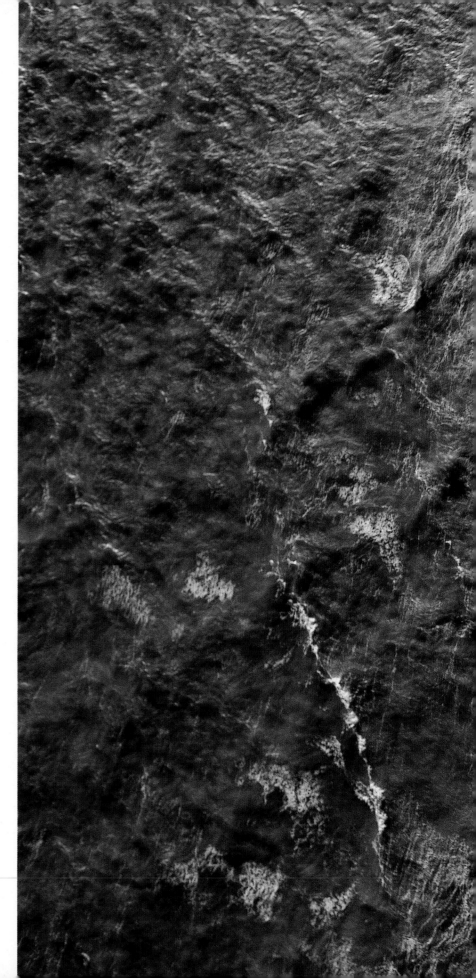

Portland Bill, Dorset

The Island of Portland is joined to mainland Dorset
by a thin strip of land at the south-eastern tip of
Chesil Beach, just south of Weymouth. It was known
as the 'Isle of Slingers' in the novels of Thomas Hardy
and is a huge slab of pale Portland limestone, which
has been quarried for use in the construction of
many well-known London buildings such as
Buckingham Palace and the British Museum.

From Portland Harbour, which was built in 1847
by convicts awaiting transportation to Australia,
the island slopes gently to the Bill, at its southern
end. Here a lighthouse and the white-painted
Trinity House Tower, built in 1844, keep watch over
treacherous waters, where tidal currents can run at
alarming speeds.

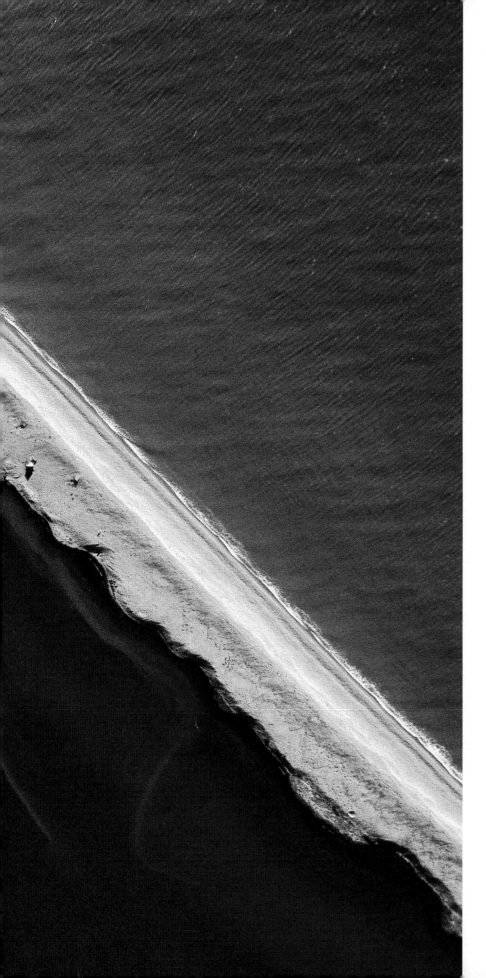

Chesil Beach, Dorset

No one really knows exactly how tidal action manages to grade the billions of pebbles along the 10 miles of Chesil Beach, but the largest ones are always found at the Portland end and the smallest at the other! The lagoon enclosed by Chesil Beach is called the Fleet and has experienced a good number of shipwrecks over the years. In 1824 a terrible gale swept the huge sloop Ebenezer into its shelter, leaving two other ships, the Carvalho and Colville, to be dashed against the beach with the loss of all hands.

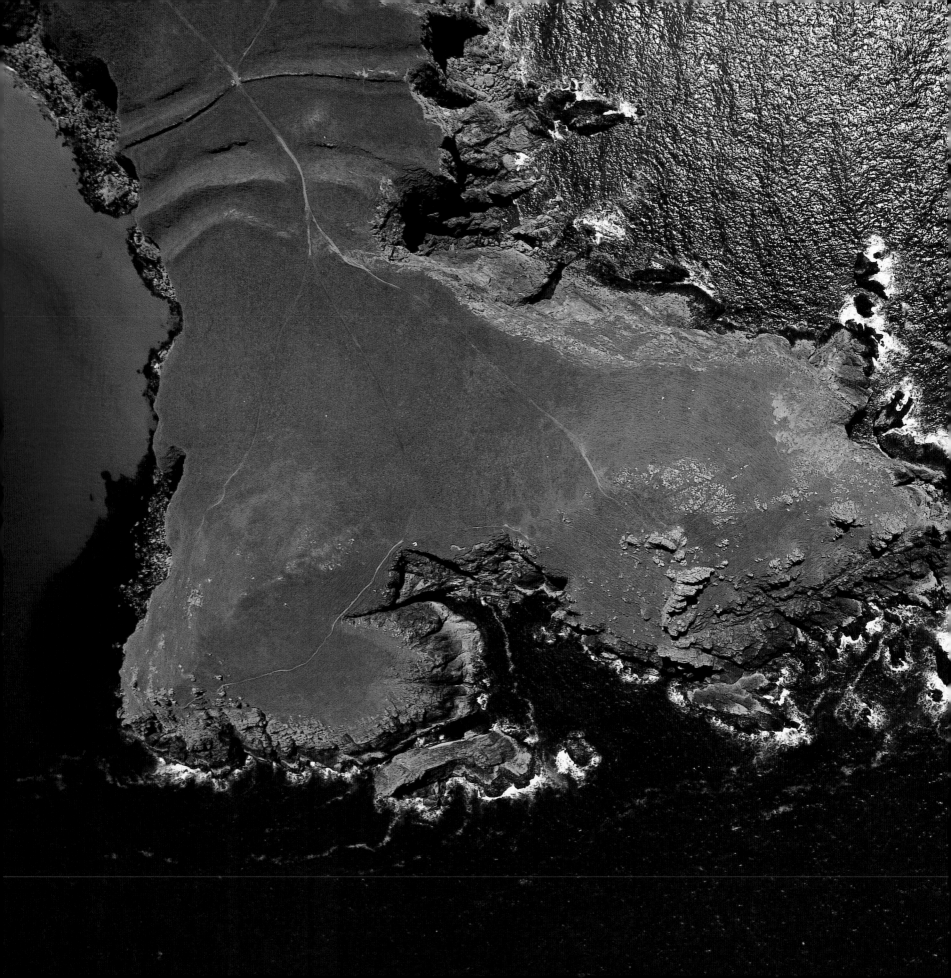

PREVIOUS PAGES

Mousehole, Cornwall

Controversy reigns over the pronunciation of the name of the picturesque fishing village on the western edge of Mount's Bay, Cornwall. Many locals maintain that it should be pronounced 'Mouzell' (rhyming with 'tousle'), whilst others say it should be pronounced as spelt. Whichever way you choose to say it, the name refers to a cave in the cliffs nearby, the Mousehole.

In the thirteenth and fourteenth centuries, Mousehole was considered to be of more maritime importance than either Penzance or Newlyn and received its first charter in 1292, some forty years earlier than that granted to Penzance. A hundred years ago it was still a bustling place, the harbour crowded with fishing boats, landing locally caught pilchards.

Rumps Point, Cornwall

Only accessible across a narrow isthmus, the fish-tail of the Rumps was recognized for its defensive potential by Iron Age man, who built a series of ditches and ramparts to make it even more impregnable. Archaeologists tell us that these early inhabitants were all but self-sufficient, weaving cloth from the wool of their sheep, harvesting the sea and cultivating grain, but it seems probable that the Rumps became deserted after the Roman invasion.

St Ives, Cornwall

St Ives is probably one of the best-known holiday towns in Cornwall. With narrow, winding cobbled streets and passages, a magnificent harbour, and superb beaches, it has become a popular haunt for tourists. In times gone by, the town relied upon pilchard fishing rather than tourism for its living. These days open boats still ply the wide sweep of St Ives Bay for mackerel, landing them late morning ready for shipment to other parts of the country.

Tintagel, Cornwall

Legend has it that King Arthur was born at Tintagel
Castle, beneath which is the cave of Merlin, the
wizard who helped the young King to become a brave
and respected ruler. Set on a small island above a
wild and wave-lashed Atlantic coast, the castle was
built in 1145 and shares its island stronghold with a
Celtic monastery of a much earlier date.

Lands End, Cornwall

Once a wild and remote spot, much of Lands End, the
most westerly point of the English mainland, is now
a theme park, attracting hundreds of thousands of
visitors every year. Looking out to sea from here gives
one an idea of the scale of the vast Atlantic Ocean,
which seems to stretch beyond the horizon for ever.
The combination of the power of the sea and the
strength of the high granite cliffs reduces man to a
mere spectator of nature.

Camel Estuary, Cornwall

The River Camel drains the western edge of Bodmin Moor, flowing from near Camelford down to the tidal waters of its estuary, which stretches from Wadebridge to the sea between Stepper and Pentire Points. The salt marsh and mudflats not only provide picturesque scenery in this estuary, but are also an important habitat for wading birds. The patient and observant visitor may also be rewarded by a sighting of an otter, especially in the early morning.

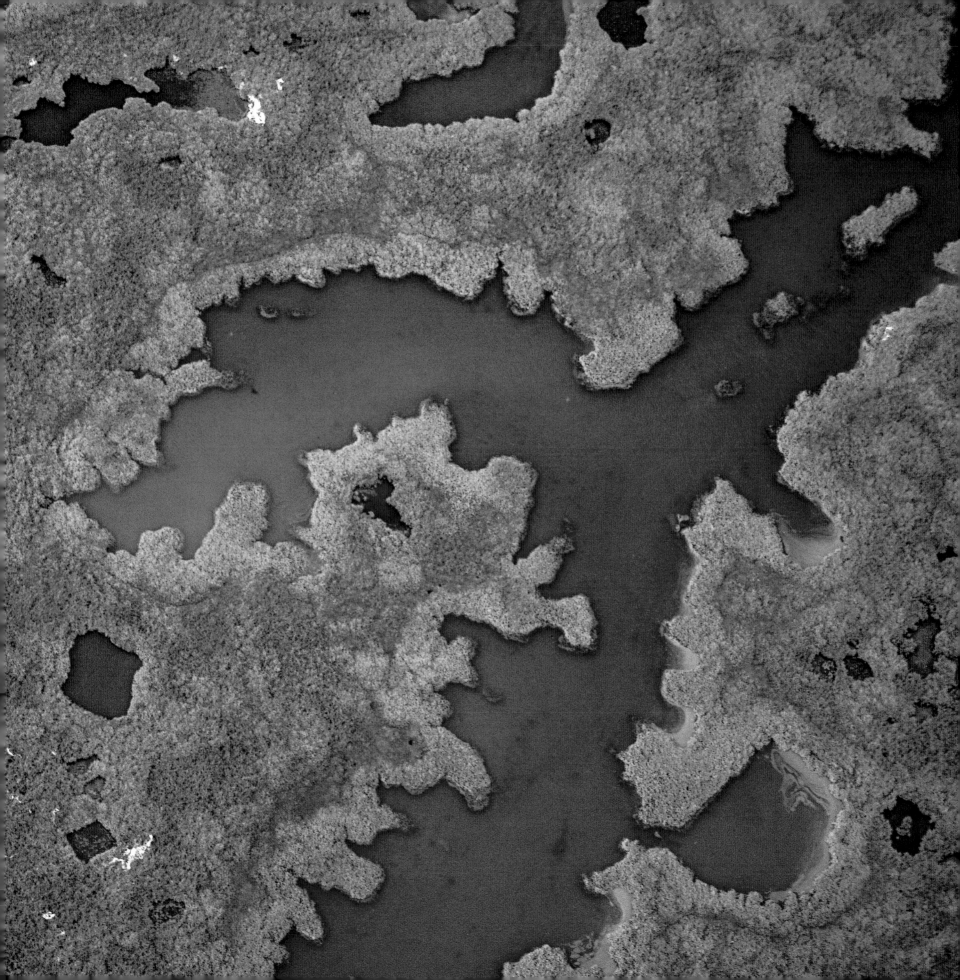

Newquay Beach, Cornwall

It was the Bishop of Exeter who sanctioned the building of a 'new quay' on the north Cornish coast in 1439, probably to capitalize on the huge shoals of pilchard in this area. In the centuries that followed, Newquay gained its wealth from fishing and smuggling but it was the coming of the railways in 1875 that transformed the town into one of the largest holiday resorts in Cornwall.

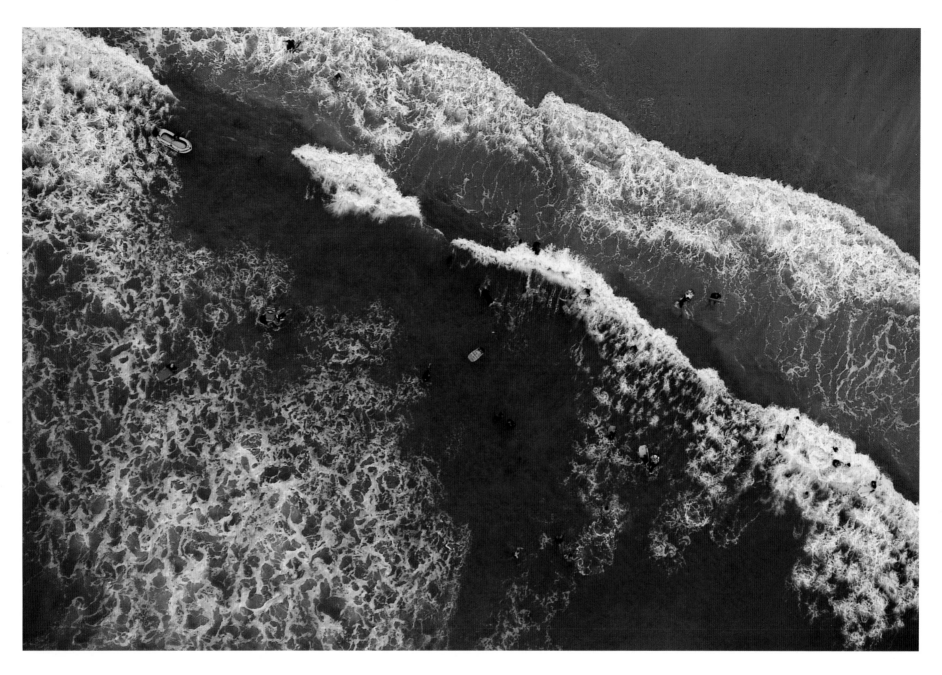

Surfers at Newquay, Cornwall

Newquay has become the surfing capital of Britain.
The large Atlantic breakers have sufficiently long
runs to make riding their crests a possibility.

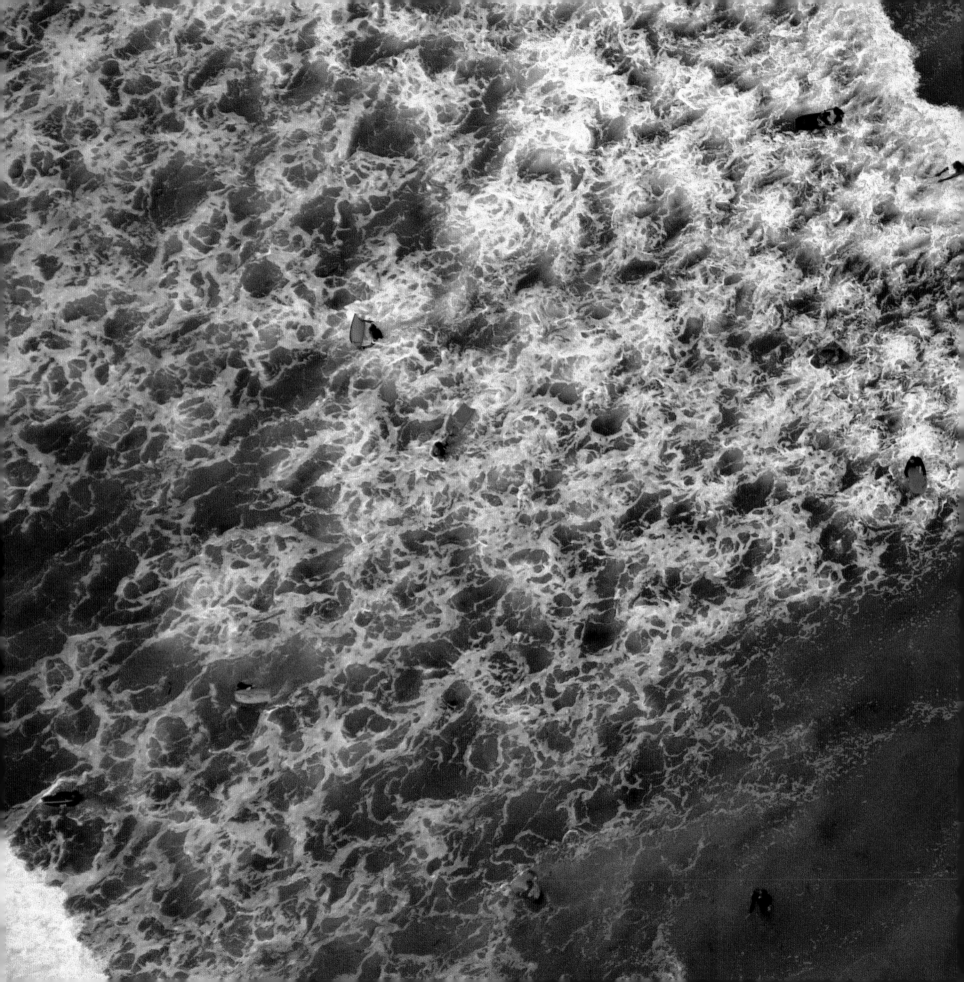

PREVIOUS PAGES
Surfers out at sea off Newquay, Cornwall
Experienced surfers do not even need a beach in
order to pursue their sport. They paddle out way
beyond the shore to ride waves that would equal
those anywhere in the world.

Newquay Beach, Cornwall
The ritual of beach life has been tried and tested
by many generations of British holidaymakers,
undeterred by the odd gale or lack of sun!

Padstow Harbour, Cornwall
St Petroc sailed from Wales in order to set up a monastery at Padstow in the sixth century. It was sacked by Viking invaders in 981 and, in medieval times, was granted the 'right of sanctuary' by King Athelstan. This enabled criminals to remain safe from arrest, and the right of sanctuary continued until the time of the Reformation. In modern times it has become well known for the culinary delights offered by the town's best-known resident, Rick Stein.

LEFT

Minack Theatre at Porthcurno, Cornwall

Built in the style of an ancient Roman amphitheatre, but with the added drama of the ocean as its backdrop, the Minack Theatre was constructed in the 1930s as a 'garden project' by Rowena Cade, who lived in the large house just behind the theatre. It has developed into a world-famous venue and has an annual summer season of plays and musical entertainment.

BELOW LEFT

Tate at St Ives, Cornwall

Tate St Ives is part of the Tate gallery in London and was opened in 1993. The gallery's inspirational building stands high above the magnificent surfing beach of Porthmeor. The Barbara Hepworth Museum, which is also part of Tate, is a lasting memorial to the great sculptress who lived and worked in St Ives.

RIGHT

Polperro, Cornwall

Polperro is a maze of lanes, alleyways and slate-hung whitewashed houses, leading down to a picturesque and unspoilt harbour. Still a working port, boats unload their catch at high tide, with pots and nets lying about the quays to add to the timeless atmosphere of the south-east Cornish harbour.

BELOW RIGHT

Falmouth, Cornwall

Fearing invasion, Henry VIII ordered two castles to be built to guard the entrance to Falmouth Harbour, forming part of his south coast defences. On the west side is Pendennis Castle, with St Mawes Castle to the east. Falmouth's heyday came in the seventeenth century when fast, packet sailing boats began carrying mail and expensive cargo to and from places as far afield as the East Indies and Spain. In 1805 it was the Falmouth Packet that brought the first news of Nelson's victory at the Battle of Trafalgar back to this country.

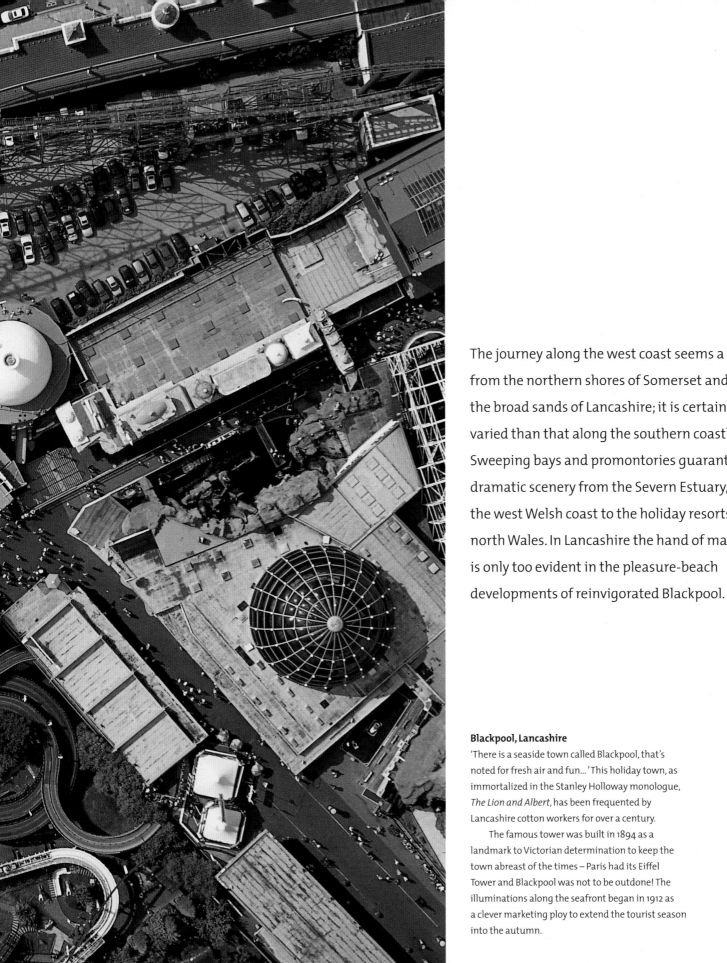

The journey along the west coast seems a long one, from the northern shores of Somerset and Avon to the broad sands of Lancashire; it is certainly no less varied than that along the southern coastline. Sweeping bays and promontories guarantee dramatic scenery from the Severn Estuary, along the west Welsh coast to the holiday resorts of north Wales. In Lancashire the hand of man is only too evident in the pleasure-beach developments of reinvigorated Blackpool.

Blackpool, Lancashire

'There is a seaside town called Blackpool, that's noted for fresh air and fun...' This holiday town, as immortalized in the Stanley Holloway monologue, *The Lion and Albert*, has been frequented by Lancashire cotton workers for over a century.

The famous tower was built in 1894 as a landmark to Victorian determination to keep the town abreast of the times – Paris had its Eiffel Tower and Blackpool was not to be outdone! The illuminations along the seafront began in 1912 as a clever marketing ploy to extend the tourist season into the autumn.

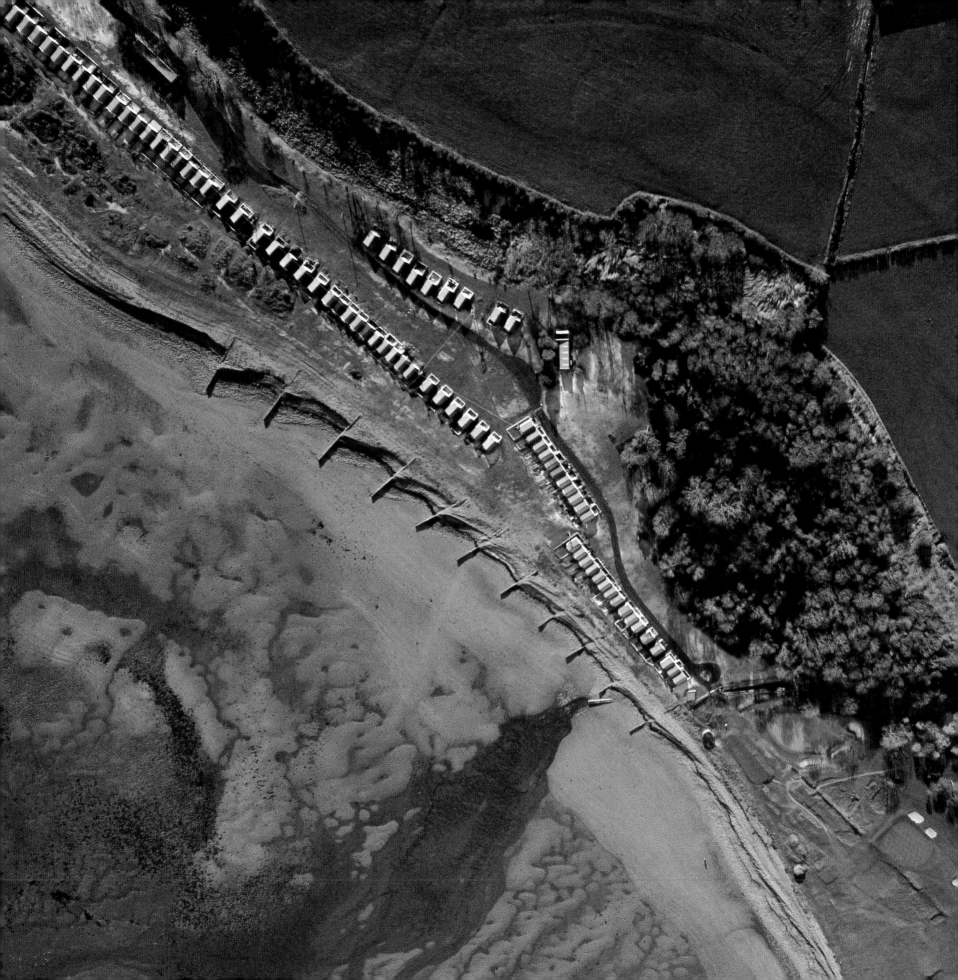

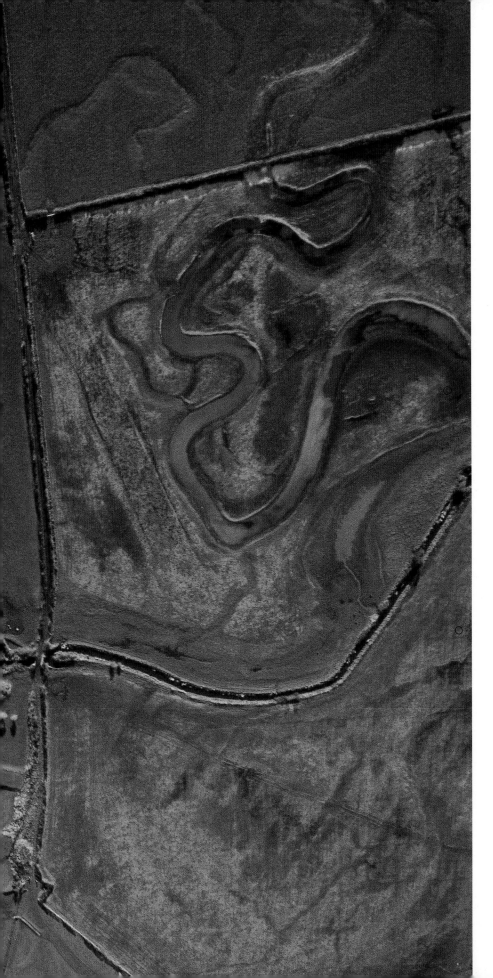

Dunster Beach, Somerset

The glorious expanses of Exmoor surround the historic village of Dunster, which is dominated by its Norman Castle. Not far away is Dunster Beach, a very small and often neglected cove, between Minehead and Blue Anchor Bay. This stream-crossed area of sand and shingle, with its golf course and row of beach huts, can be a challenge to bathers as the tide goes out more than half a mile!

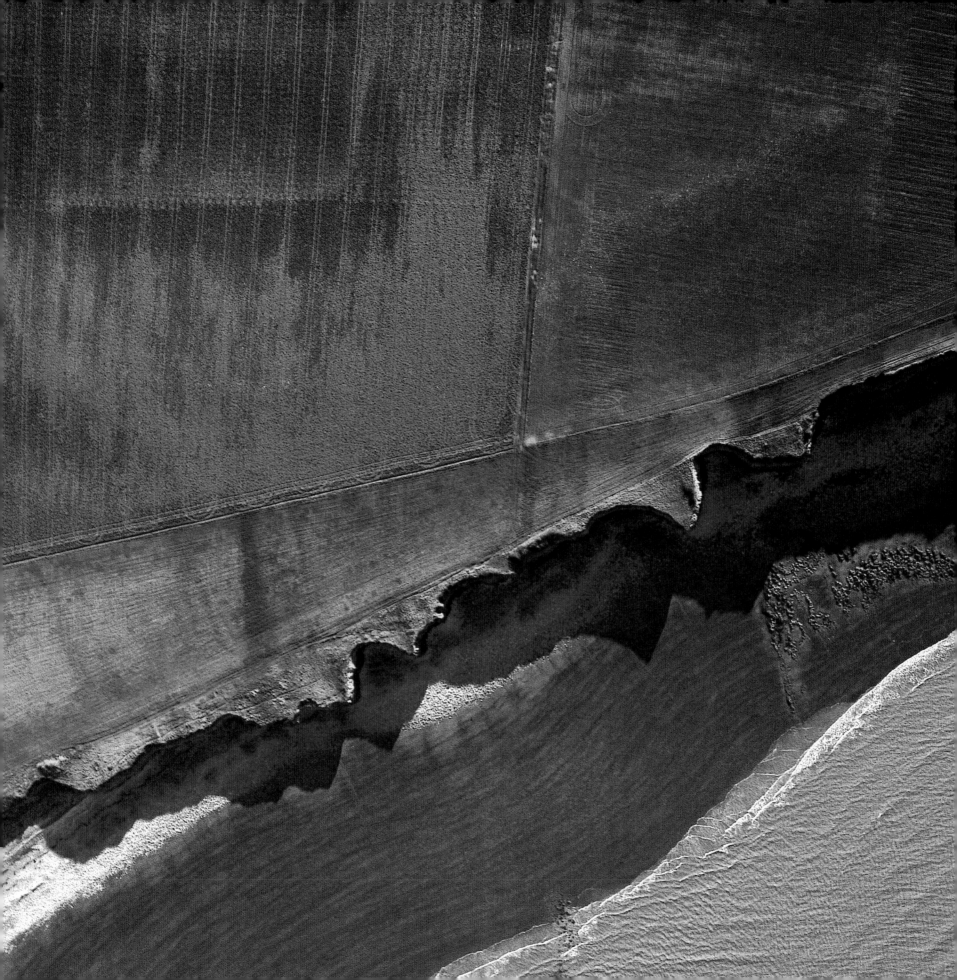

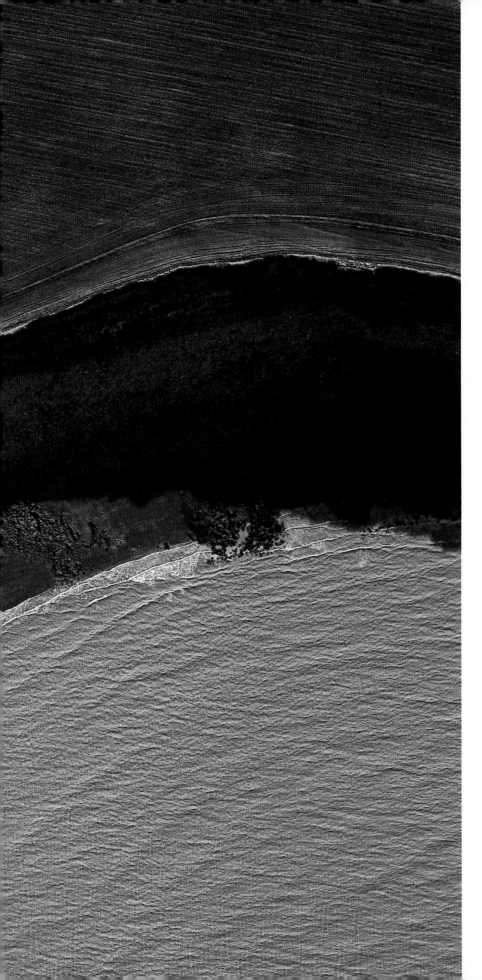

Cliffs near East Quantoxhead, Somerset
Low, crumbling cliffs mark the start of the Quantock
Hills, which were Britain's first designated Area of
Outstanding Natural Beauty. The view over the
Bristol Channel is spectacular, with the islands of
Steep Holm and Flat Holm, Brean Down, at the tip
of the Mendips, and the Welsh coast clearly visible
from here.

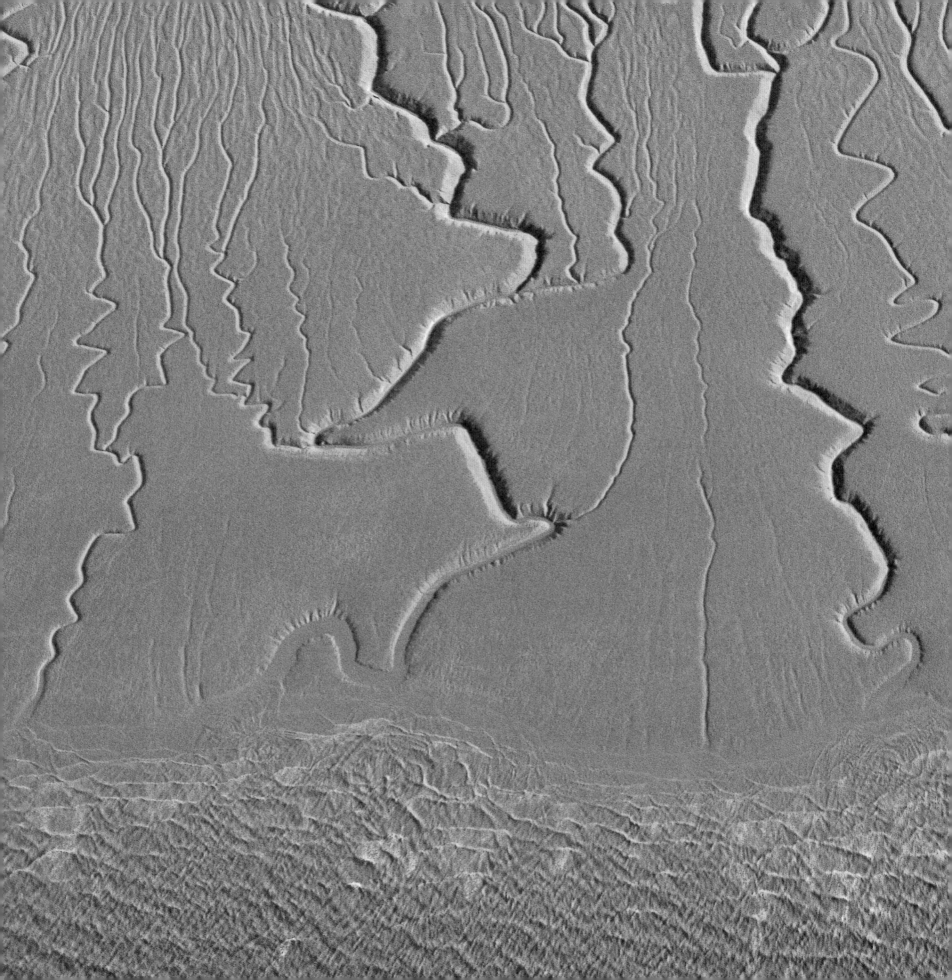

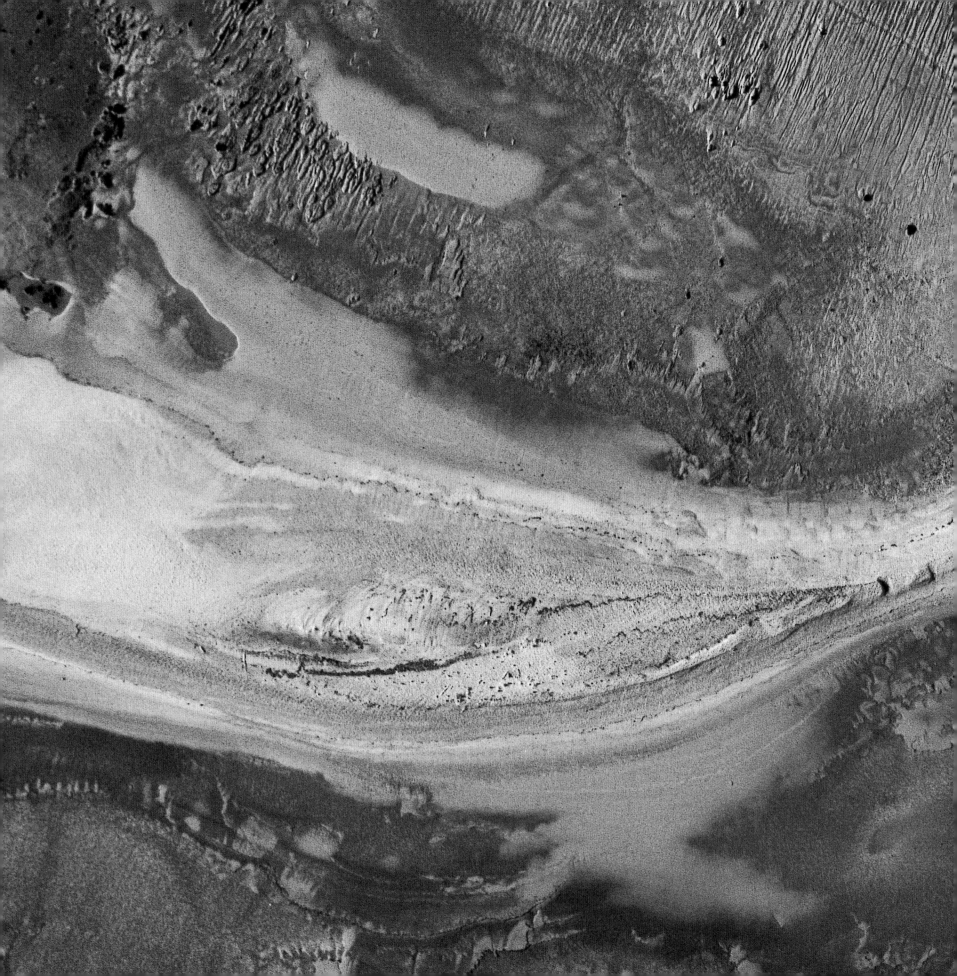

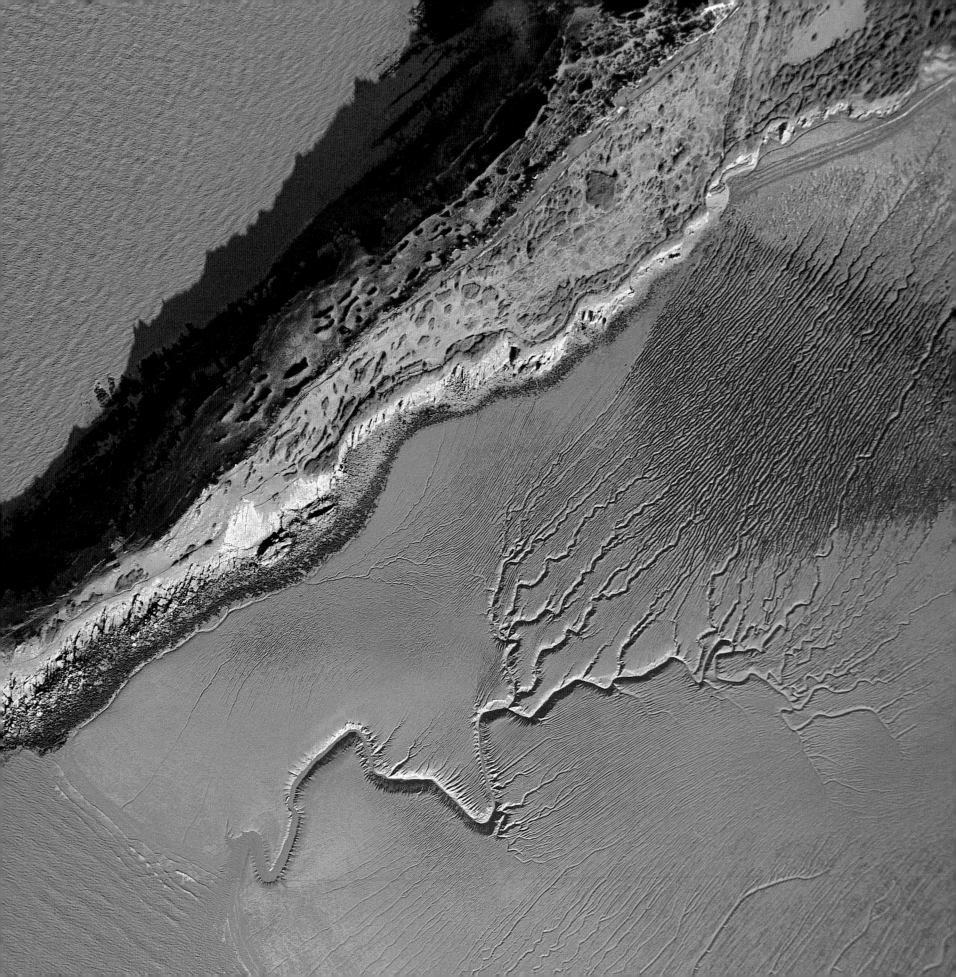

Sand Bay, Somerset

The strange veins, which appear in relief when the sand dries out at low tide, are a good example of a raised beach that was possibly formed half a million years ago, when the sea level was different. Sand Bay is the northern beach of the popular seaside town of Weston-super-Mare, which is said to be everything that a Victorian seaside resort should be, complete with genteel stone villas, two piers, museum and aquarium.

Sand Point, Somerset

Sand Point is a narrow limestone cliff with outcrops of rock at the northern end of Sand Bay. This is a popular area with birdwatchers and rare visitors such as the bee-eater, hoopoe, wryneck and tawny pipit have been seen here.

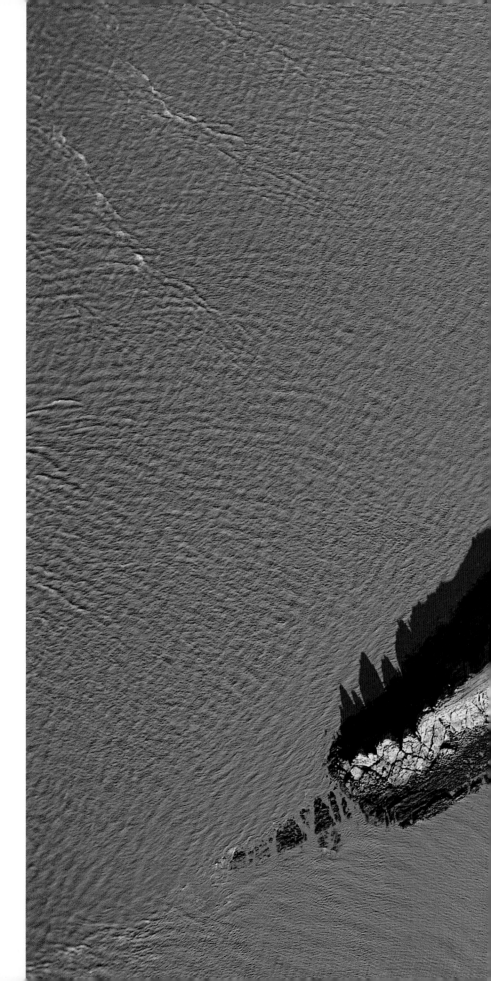

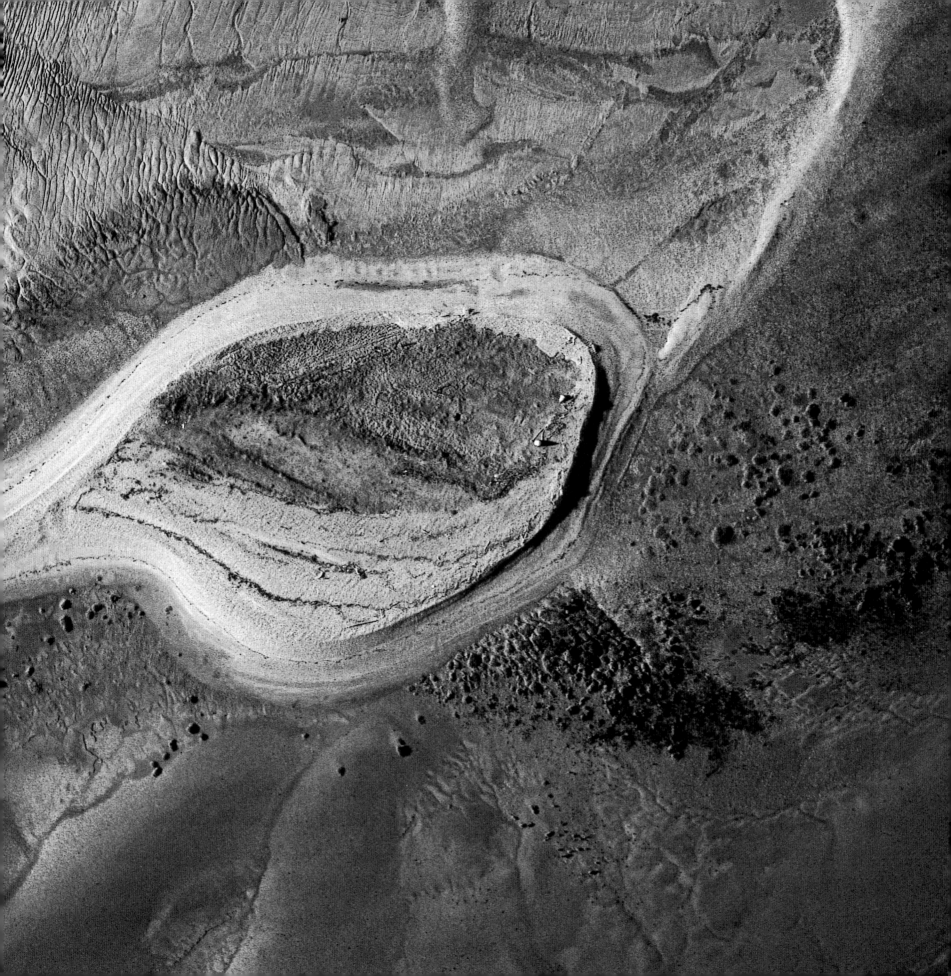

Severn Estuary, West Coast

The tides which sweep up and down the lower reaches of the River Severn's wide estuary can rise and fall more than 17 metres at their height. These swirling currents make ever-changing patterns in the mud and shoreline.

Blackstone Rocks, Somerset

The area around Clevedon, on the Somerset shore of the Bristol Channel, is rich in archaeology. Here Mesolithic flint tools have been found on Blackstone Rocks just off the mainland.

Berrow Flats, Somerset

Berrow Flats sweep down from Brean Down to
the south of Weston-super-Mare to the mouth
of the River Parrett at Burnham-on-Sea. The remains
of a Norwegian ship which foundered in 1897 can be
seen here.

BELOW LEFT

Blue Ben, St Audries Bay, Somerset

Going down to St Audries Bay by way of a zigzag
pathway adds to the drama of this magnificent
section of the Somerset coastline. Once on the
beach and past the waterfall, both sides of the bay
can be observed to breath-taking effect. Looking
east the headland named Blue Ben is visible; here
ammonites are very common within the
alternating layers of black shale.

Lleyn Peninsula, Wales

The Lleyn Peninsula is usually defined as the strip of land from Caernarfon to Porthmadog and is where the mountains of Snowdonia meet the sea. From the heights of Yr Eifl to the sandy shores of Abersoch, this Area of Outstanding Natural Beauty is one of the most beautiful areas in Wales.

BELOW RIGHT

Near Porthmadog, Wales

The harbour town of Porthmadog is rich in maritime history. The town was named after W. A. Maddocks whose ambitious 'Cob' embankment scheme led to the town's name, which translates as 'Madog's Port'. In times gone by, it was a vital, busy shipping port for the international slate trade, brought down from Blaenau Ffestiniog by the famous Ffestiniog Light Railway.

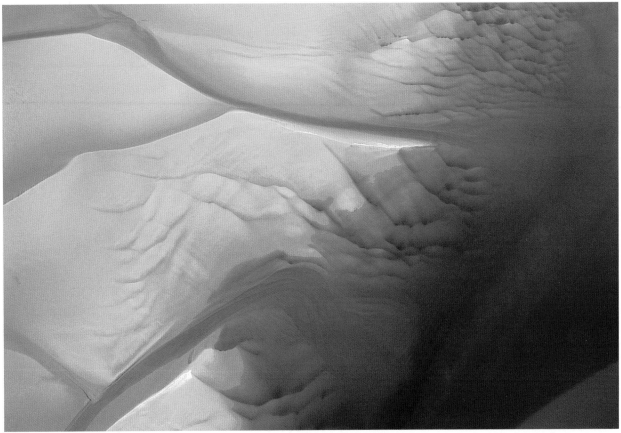

Ynyslas, Borth, Wales

Ynyslas means 'green-blue island' in Welsh. It is thought that the dunes at Ynyslas have been forming since the thirteenth century. The dunes form when strong, dry winds blow from the north-west, bringing sand onshore from sand bars at the entrance to the Dyfi Estuary, which are exposed at low water.

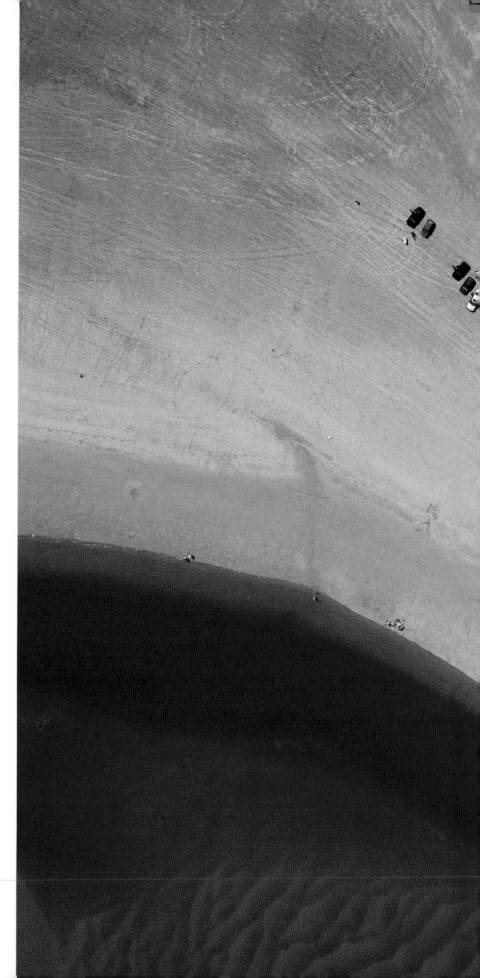

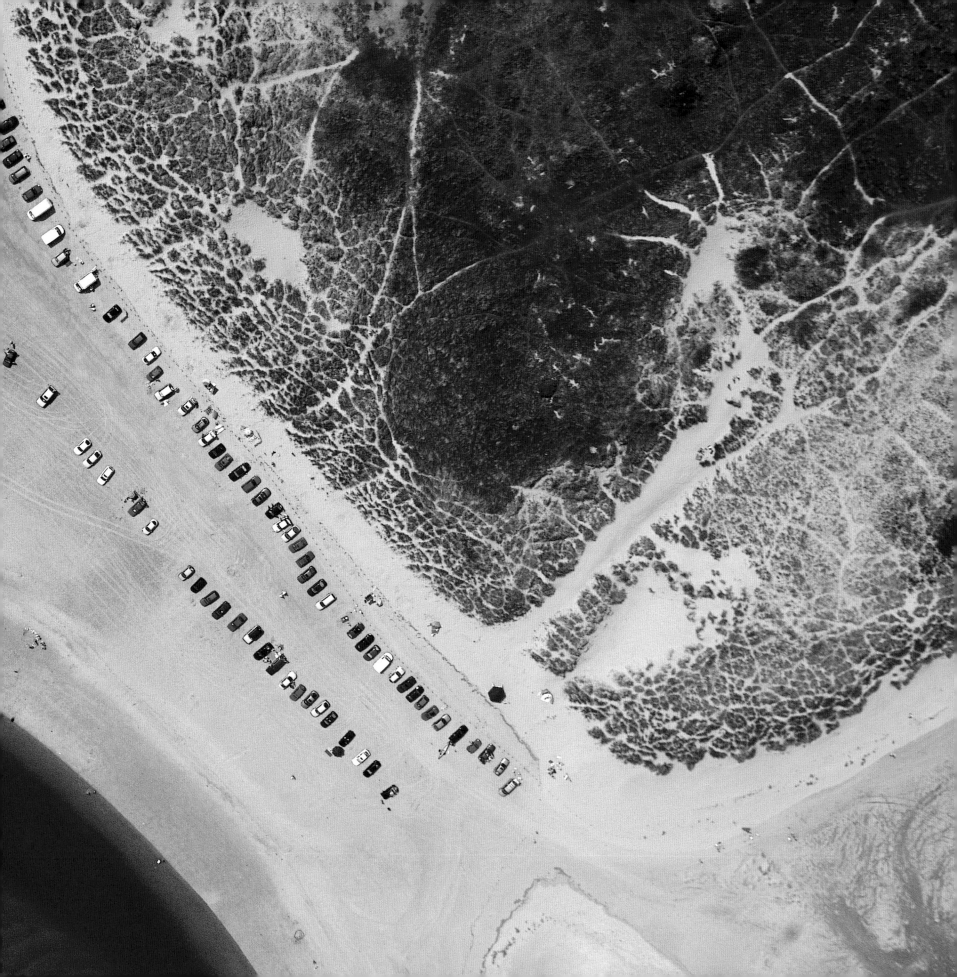

Estuary of the Afon Dwyryd, Wales
Close to Porthmadog is Portmeirion, with its unique and famous Italianate village built by the architect Sir Clough Williams-Ellis. This small town became famous as the set for the television series *The Prisoner*, starring Patrick McGoohan.

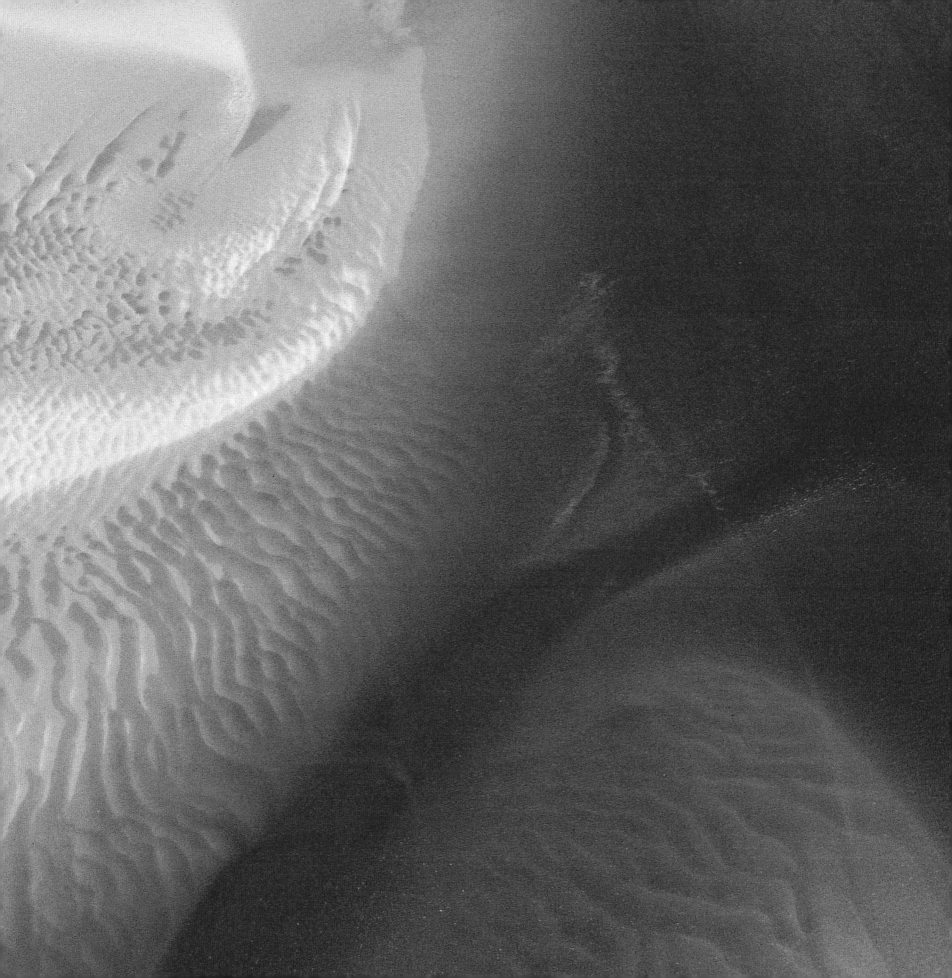

PREVIOUS PAGES
Lleyn Peninsula, Wales

In terms of both landscape and weather, the Lleyn Peninsula is very different to the rest of Wales. Much of Lleyn is rolling countryside, rising up to the occasional volcanic peak.

Conwy Castle and Bridges, Wales

The dark-stoned fortress of Conwy Castle dominates one of the best-preserved fortified towns in Britain. Its circuit of walls, over three quarters of a mile long and guarded by no less than twenty-two towers, is one of the finest in the world. Close by are three bridges that cross the River Conwy, which combine with the castle and town walls to make an unforgettable skyline.

Caernarfon, Wales

Caernarfon is architecturally one of the most impressive castles in Wales. During Edward I's campaign into Wales, this was a strategically excellent place to build a castle. Anglesey, often referred to as 'the garden of Wales', provided rich land close to the poorer land of north Wales. The Menai Strait also allowed speedy access between the north Welsh coast and the western coast. It was here that Prince Charles was invested as Prince of Wales on 1 July, 1969.

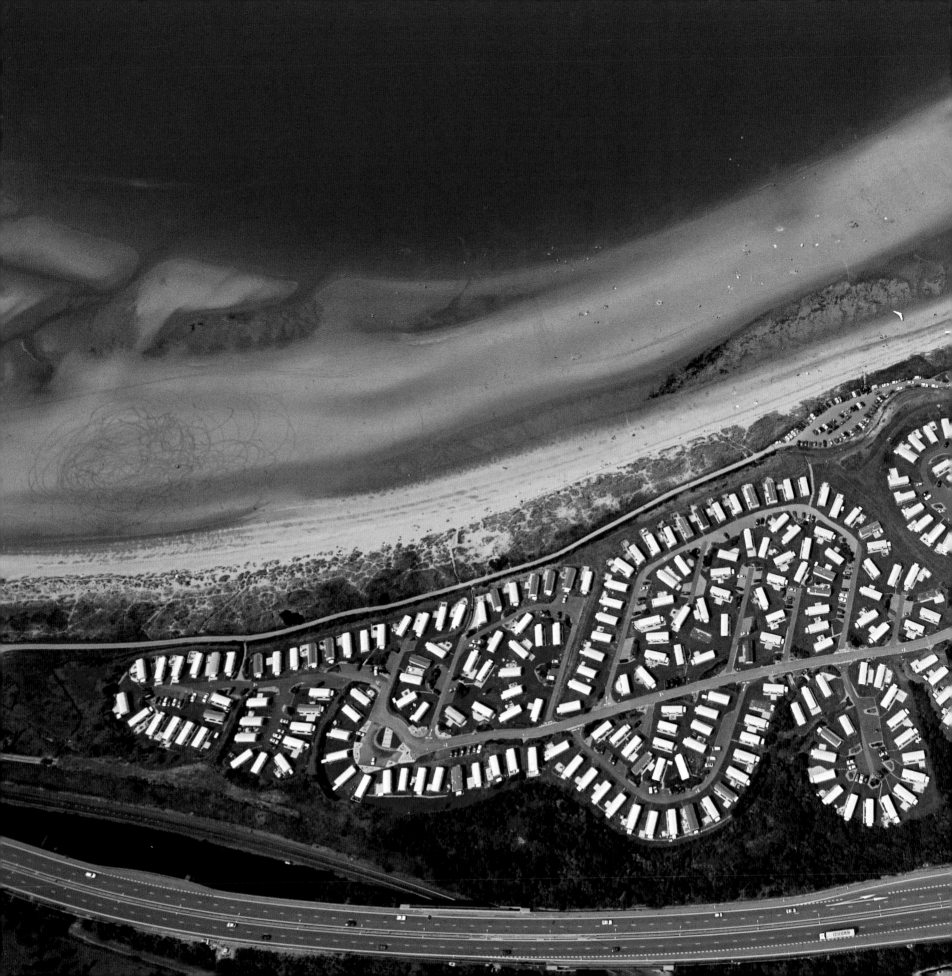

Conwy Morfa, Wales

The entire north coast of Wales, from Prestatyn to Bangor, is littered with caravan sites: a testament to the popularity of this section of the British coastline as a holiday resort. But Conwy Morfa not only has caravans, it also holds a secret. The 'Mulberry Harbours' which were used in World War II to assist with the D-Day landings were built here amidst great secrecy. These floating barriers were designed to act as a harbour and enable vast supplies of equipment, stores and men to be brought ashore on the French coast quickly.

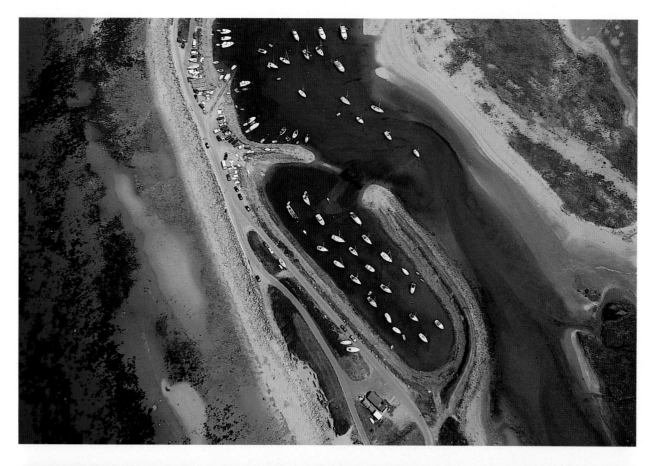

LEFT
Llandanwg and Shell Island, Wales

The shifting sand dunes on the edge of the River Artro Estuary have half-buried much of the old village of Llandanwg, including the church. This inundation of sand was no doubt accelerated by the Earl of Winchester in the early years of the nineteenth century. He decided to increase the area of his estate at Llandanwg by diverting the River Artro and reclaiming the land. Where once there had been a river, new sand dunes appeared and, because of the peculiarities of the offshore currents, the peninsular became covered in shells of more than two hundred kinds. It thus got its name of 'Shell Island'.

BELOW LEFT
Power Boat, Wales

The exhilarating feeling of skimming across the water at high speed attracts many people to speed-boating. The sensation of the wind and sea spray in your face and the adrenaline rush provided by the power boats make this a popular sport in Britain.

Conwy Estuary, Wales

The spectacular backdrop of Snowdonia and the magical medieval town of Conwy, with its castle and bridges, make the Conwy Estuary one of the most popular in Wales.

Paddling Pool at Llandudno, Wales

With seas that were frequently too rough or polluted to permit sea bathing, an early twentieth century innovation was the introduction of the 'lido' or open-air swimming pool and paddling pools for younger children. Like this pool at Llandudno, lidos were promoted for the cleanliness of their water, which was constantly refreshed. These pools were often embellished with fountains and cascades, slides and diving platforms, as well as being surrounded by terraces for sunbathing, cafés and other facilities.

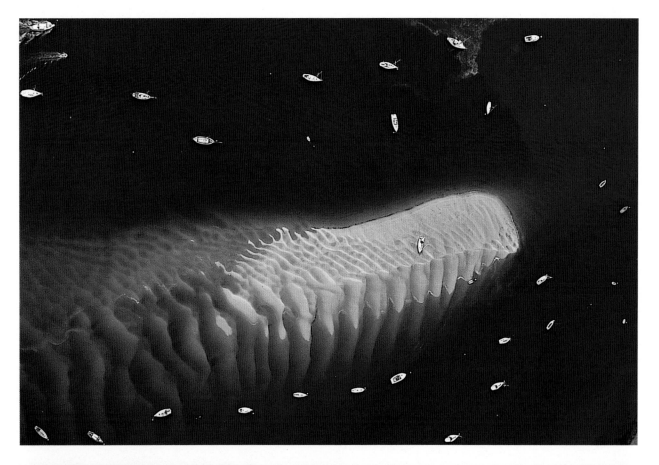

Llandudno, Wales

Between two notable carboniferous headlands, the Great Orme and Little Orme, with the Irish Sea on one side and the estuary of the River Conwy on the other, lies the seaside town of Llandudno. Laid out by Edward Mostyn and Owen Williams in the mid-nineteenth century with well-planned streets and a wide promenade, the town has retained much of its Victorian charm.

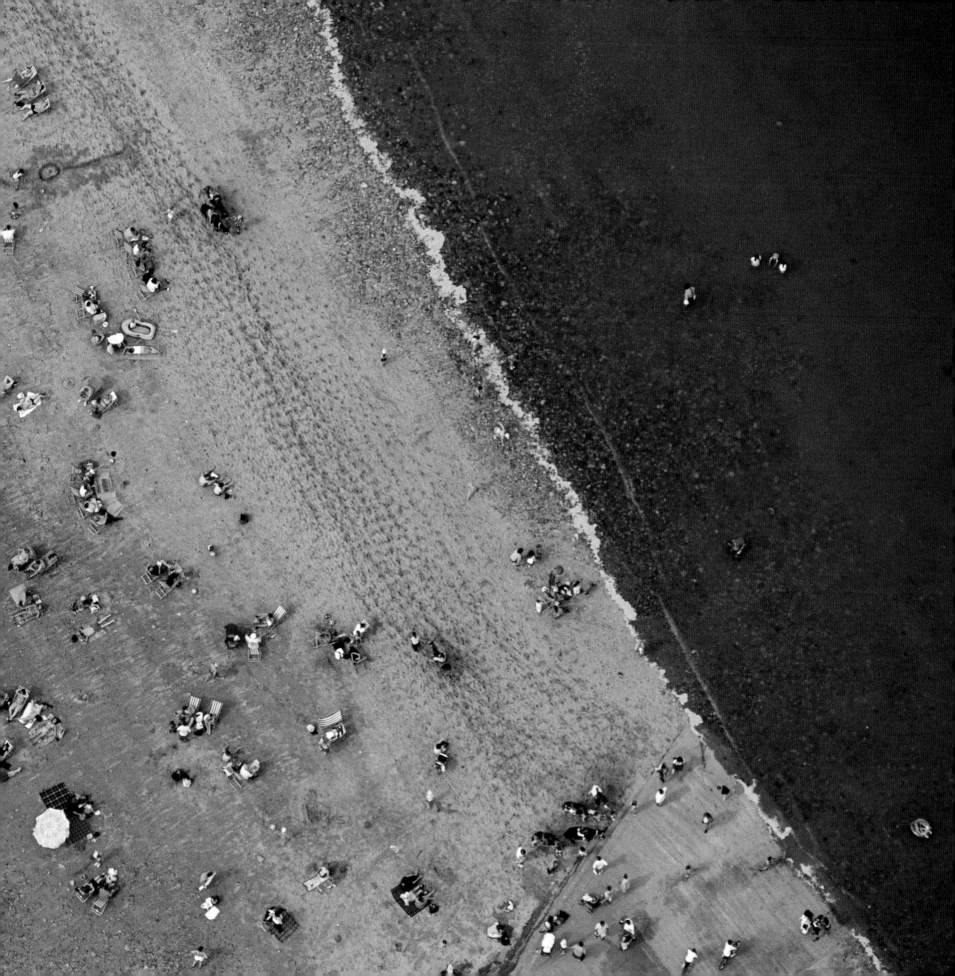

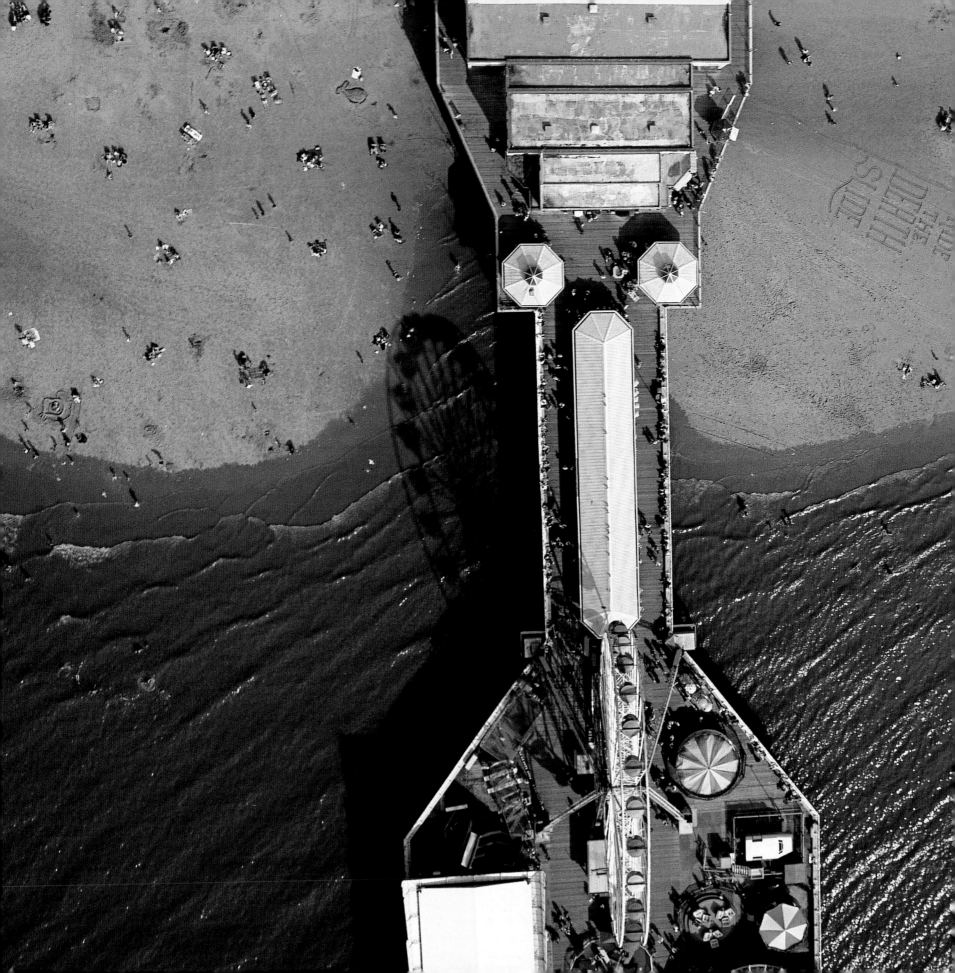

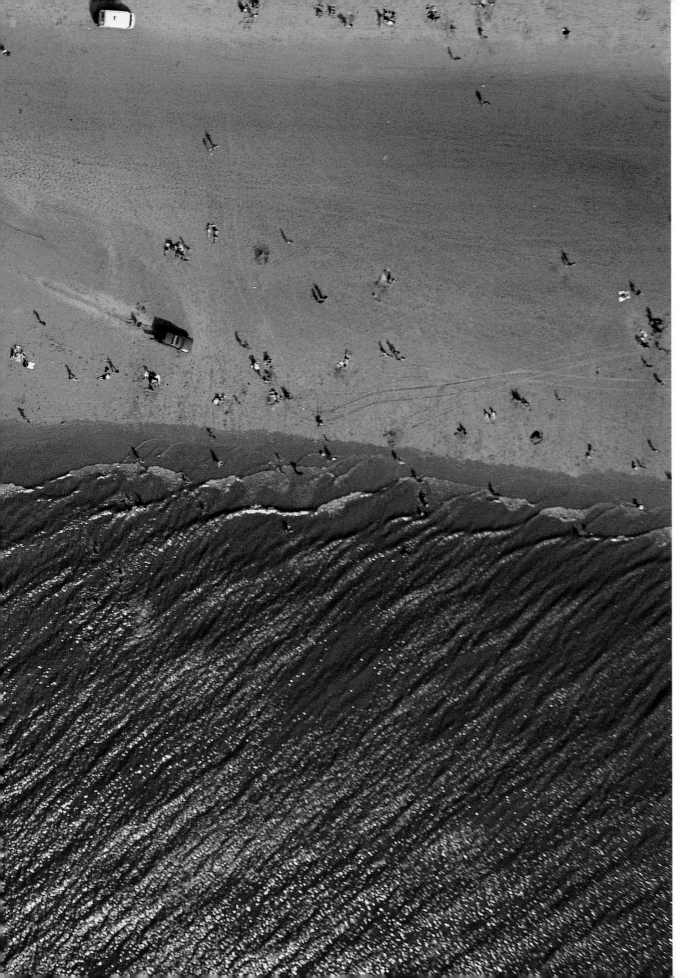

Blackpool South Pier, Lancashire

Probably the most popular source of entertainment for people on a day at the seaside is the pier. The first pier in Britain was built at Ryde on the Isle of Wight in 1814, but this was primarily a landing stage.

The first pier to be built as a leisure attraction was the Brighton Chain Pier, which opened in 1823 and marked the birth of the pleasure pier. Blackpool's South Pier, which was completed in March 1893, was very up-market and in 1894 a full orchestra and choir gave a performance of Handel's *Messiah* during the summer season.

NEXT PAGES
Blackpool Central Pier, Lancashire

As Blackpool's popularity grew in the nineteenth century, it became clear that additional facilities would be required for the increasing number of visitors. The Blackpool South Jetty Company was formed in 1864, and a design from J. I. Mawson was accepted for the new Central Pier. The Central Pier has always been considered the 'fun' pier and a roller-skating rink was opened in 1909 for an admission fee of half a penny. Further novelties to attract visitors followed, including a 'joy wheel' in 1911, speedboats and a racing car ride in 1920, a 'guess your weight' machine, photograph booth and an automatic chip dispenser in 1932.

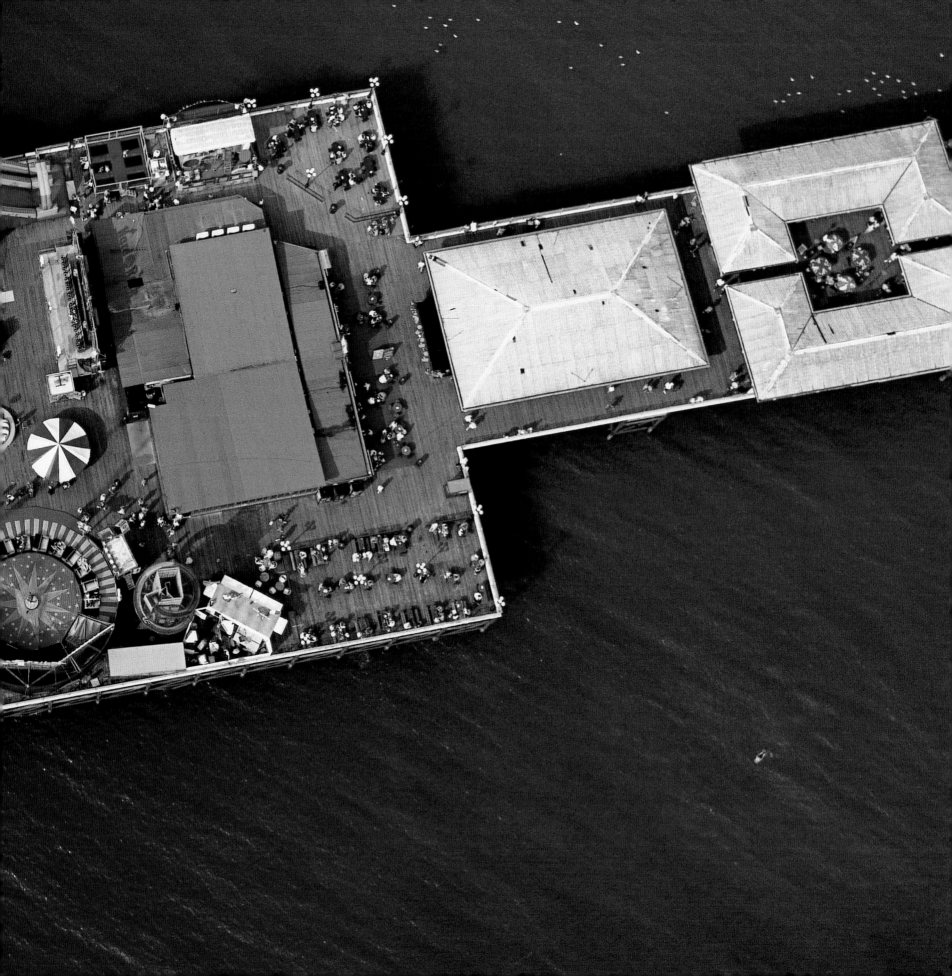

From Cape Wrath southwards through the Western Isles, and across the North Channel to Ulster, lie some of the most dramatic physical formations of the whole British coastline. Long sea lochs and numerous islands mean that there are ever-changing shades of water and land, as depths give way to shallows, and white sandy beaches alternate with the forbidding crags that descend to the shoreline. The east coast of Scotland is also varied, but human intervention is more conspicuous in the form of golf courses and small fishing harbours.

Loch a'Bhaile, Lewis, Scotland
Relentlessly battered by fierce Atlantic winds, the Hebrides can seem a hostile environment. Also known as 'Long Island', the Outer Hebrides consist of a narrow 130-mile long chain of islands, lying 40 miles off the north-west coast of Scotland. Much of the interior is bleak peat bog, rocks and endless tiny lochs.

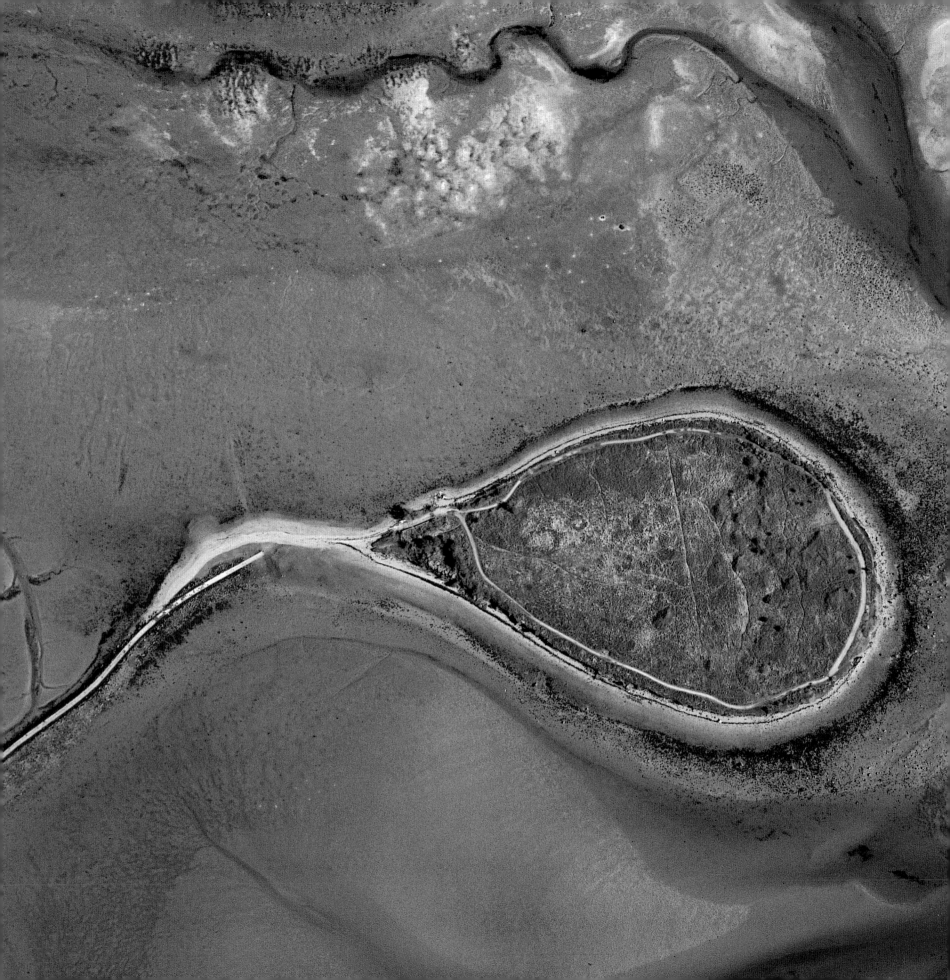

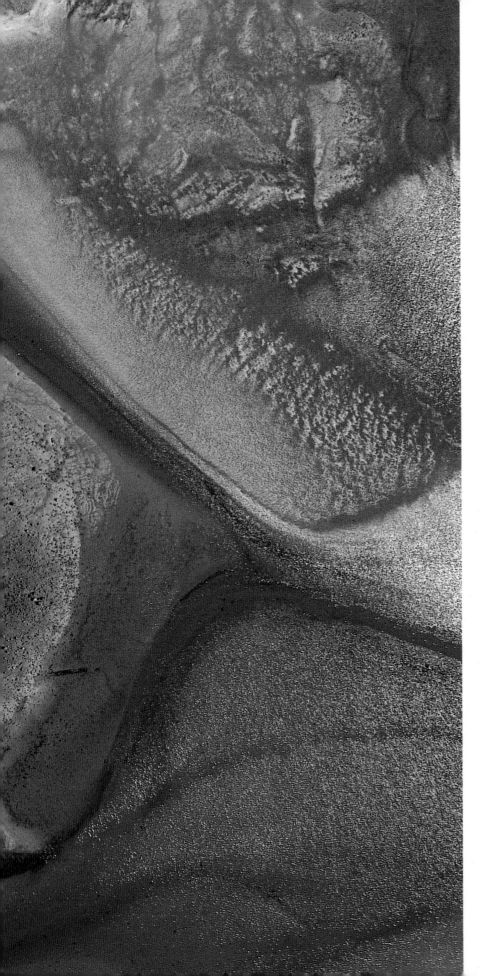

Strangford Lough, Northern Ireland

At over 20 miles long, Strangford Lough is one of the largest sea inlets in the British Isles. In places the lough is 5 miles wide, but the Narrows, where it joins the sea, form a bottleneck less than half a mile across which creates treacherous currents. St Patrick risked these currents when he sailed into the lough in AD432 to convert the country to Christianity.

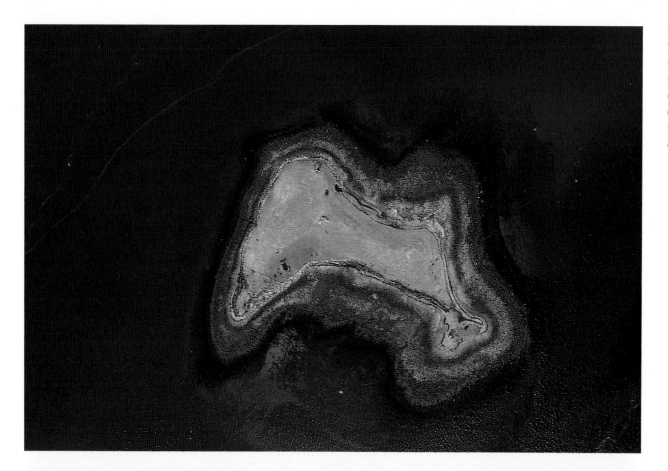

The low, flat landscape of the lough is littered with small islands that look like semi-submerged flying saucers. These islets, know as 'drumlins', are deposits dumped by the retreating ice sheet at the end of the last Ice Age. The drumlins and shoreline provide habitats for a huge variety of plants, animals and birds.

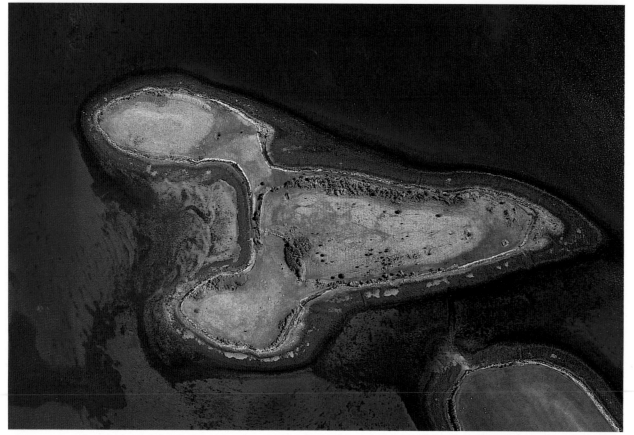

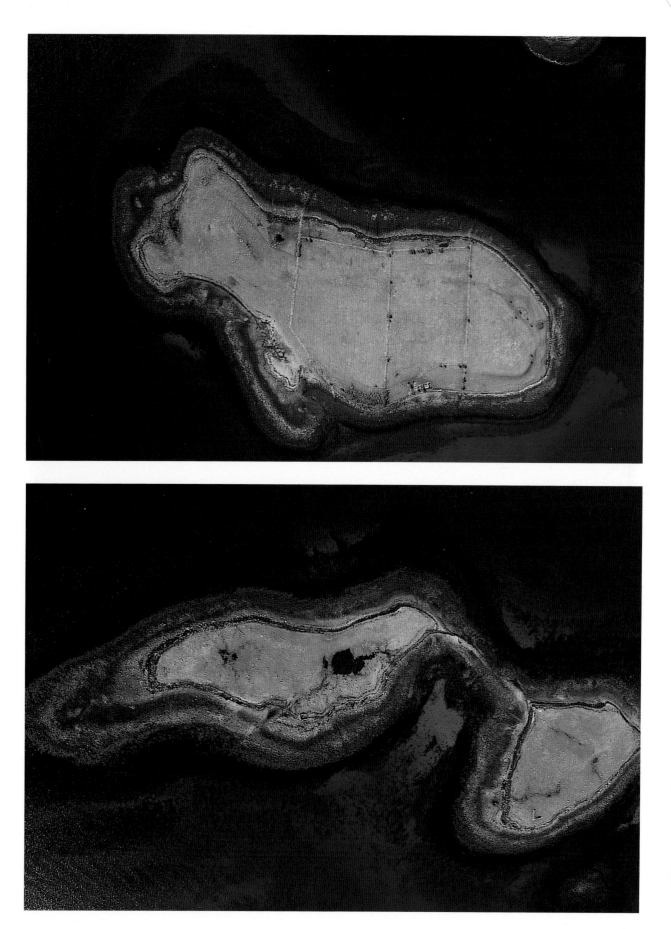

Shoreline near Ballycastle, Northern Ireland
Ballycastle is a small seaside town on the most
north-easterly tip of County Antrim, Northern
Ireland. It is surrounded by some of the most awe-
inspiring coastal scenery in Ireland, which is also
steeped in cultural history. This is the land of the
Giant's Causeway, where majestic cliffs and
inaccessible bays combine with myth and legend
to inspire. But amongst this breathtaking
landscape are echoes of another reality – isolated
ruins, kelp walls and shoreline fields bear testament
to the harder life of farming and fishing endured
by past generations.

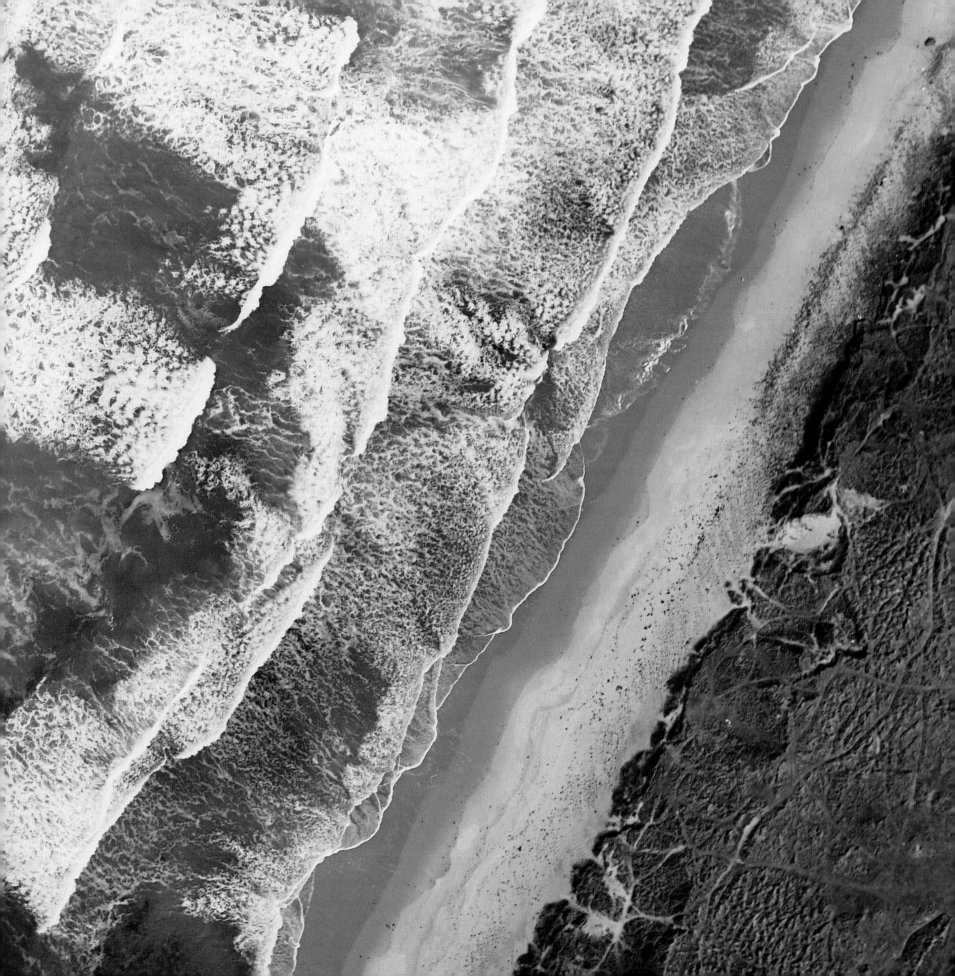

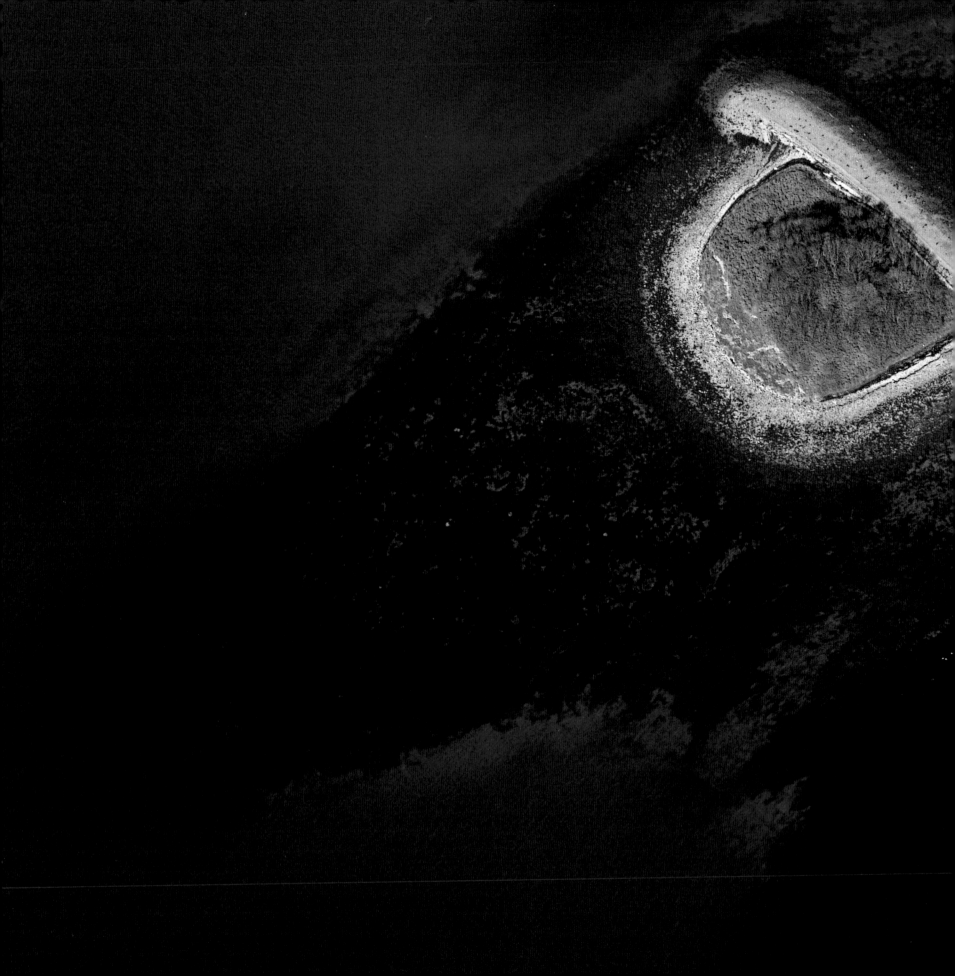

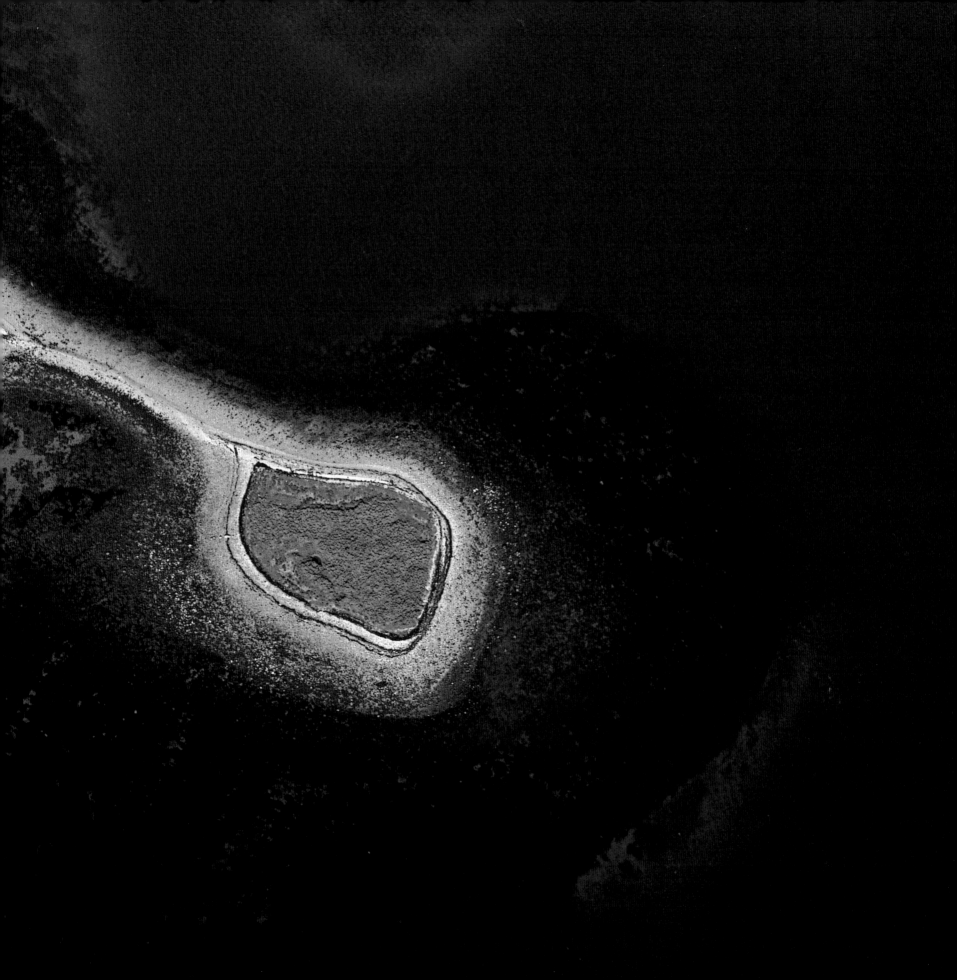

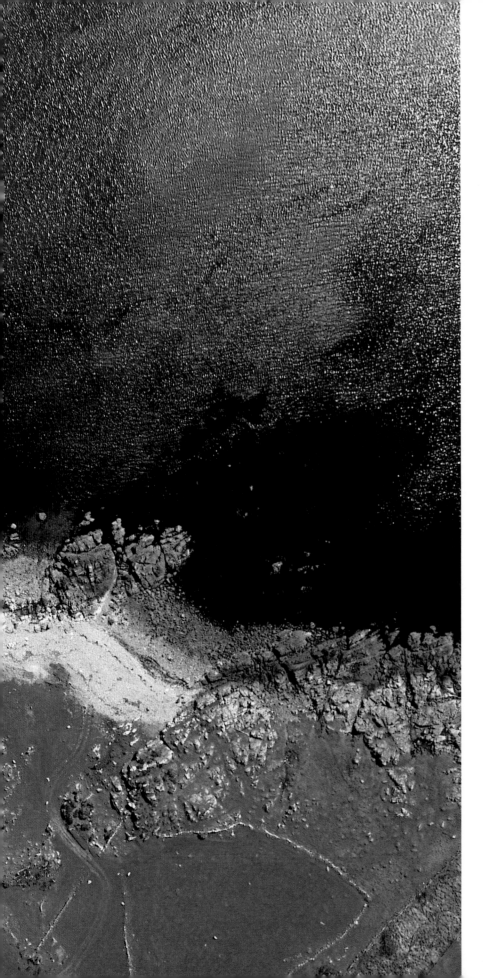

PREVIOUS PAGES

Strangford Lough, Northern Ireland

Folklore has it that there is an island for every day
of the year. Then there are the hundreds of semi-
submerged islands known as 'pladdies' – the
remains of islands long ago eroded by weather and
waves. Many of the larger drumlins show the scars
and debris of human endeavour and use. Around
one hundred and fifty kelp kilns, used to produce
soda and iodine from seaweed, have been found
on and around the lough.

County Down, Northern Ireland

The rich and varied coastline of County Down runs
from Belfast in the north to Newcastle in the south,
taking in such wonders as Murlogh, where there
is a man-made rabbit warren dating back to
Norman times.

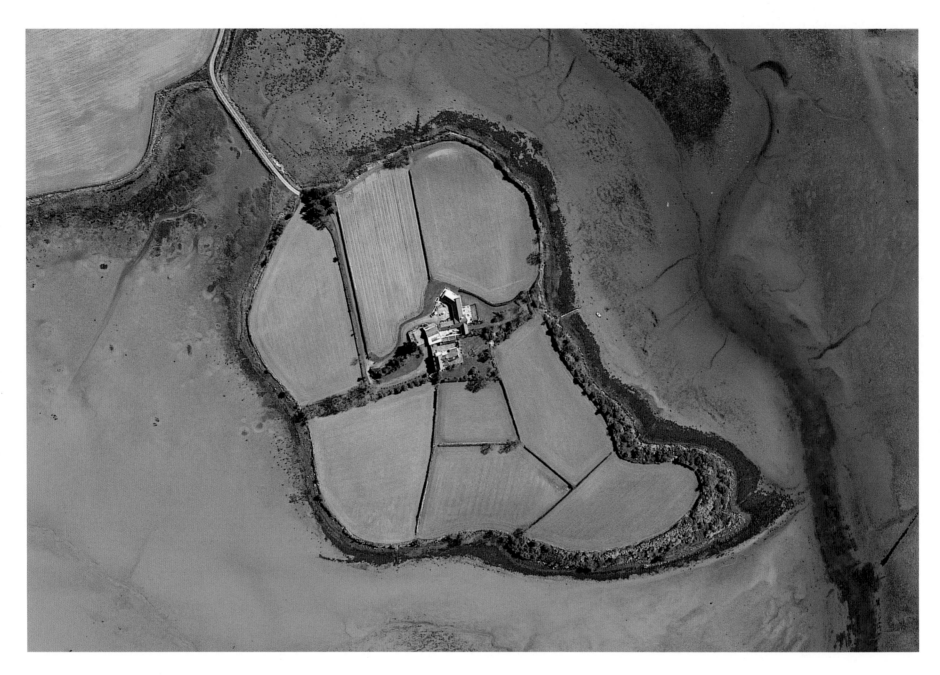

Strangford Lough, Northern Ireland

Some islands channel and funnel the retreating tide, allowing fish traps to be set, which are still evident in some places. These traps generally consist of stone walls, built in the medieval period, which superseded earlier constructions made of wood. Both constructions were designed to provide crafty fish traps which obstructed their escape following the ebbing tide. Carbon dating puts the earliest of these at around the ninth century.

Strangford Lough, Northern Ireland

The 1851 population census shows two hundred and forty-seven souls living on seventeen drumlins raising animals, crops and children. The evidence is a legacy of ridge-and-furrow which once grew potatoes and oats, stone plinths used for keeping the hay dry off the ground, ruined farmsteads and more.

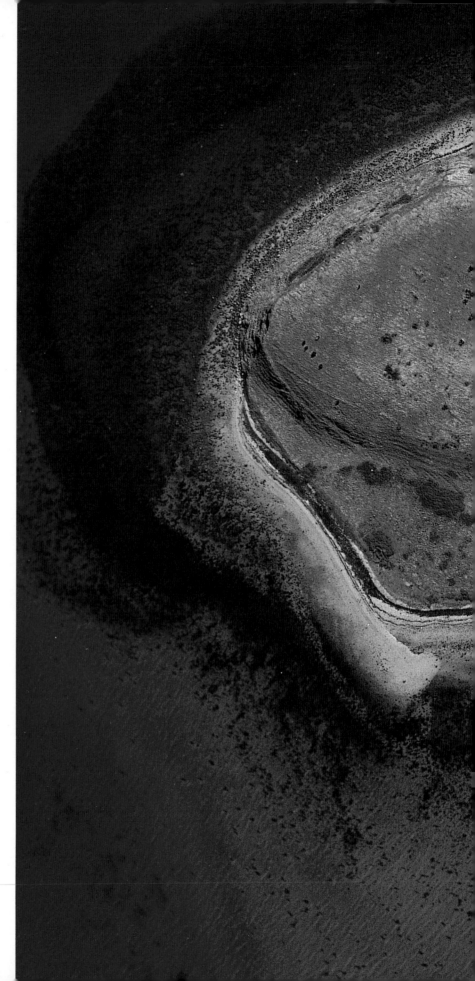

Strangford Lough, Northern Ireland
The drumlins and pladdies are significant for marine mammals, particularly the common and grey seals. They are essential to these gregarious and sociable creatures, providing birthing and nursing sites and places where they can rest between feeding forays.

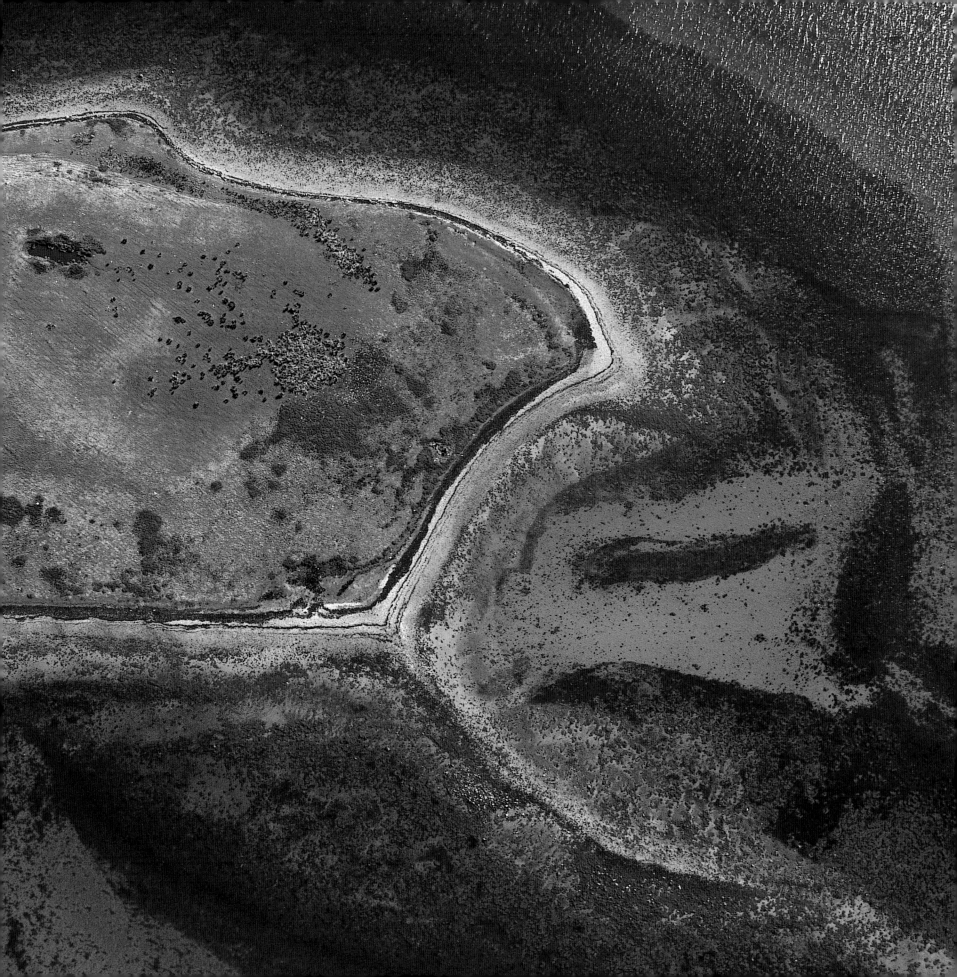

Near Larne, County Antrim, Northern Ireland
Sand bars come in many shapes and sizes,
depending on how current and wave action relates
to the bar. Constantly moving, they can be an
extreme hazard to navigation.

Near Ballycastle, Northern Ireland
The North Antrim coast is one of the most
geologically rich areas in Britain. From the volcanic
basalt of the famous Giant's Causeway to the sandy
beach and chalk cliffs of White Park Bay, this stretch
of coastline offers a wide variety of coastal forms.

NEXT PAGES
County Down, Northern Ireland
The County Down coastline has much to offer the
walker and naturalist, with a rocky shore and
heathland at Ballymacormick Point and wildfowl,
wading birds and gulls at Orlock Point.

PAGES 122–23
North Antrim Coast, Northern Ireland
The natural action of wind and tide causes
landslides and erodes soft cliffs, low-lying land,
sand dunes and salt marshes. Other areas become
silted up as new land is formed. Changing weather
conditions, tides and natural processes, such as
erosion and deposition, all contribute to the rich
and diverse landscapes and ecosystems found on
our coasts.

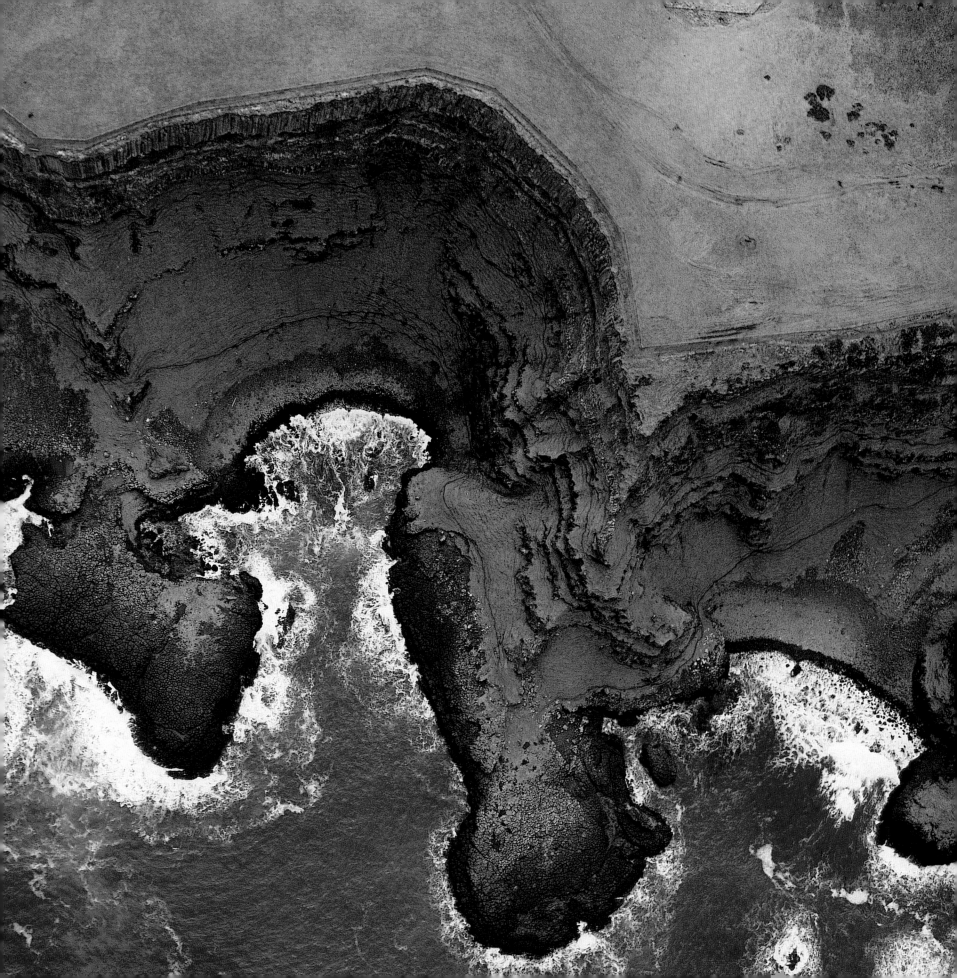

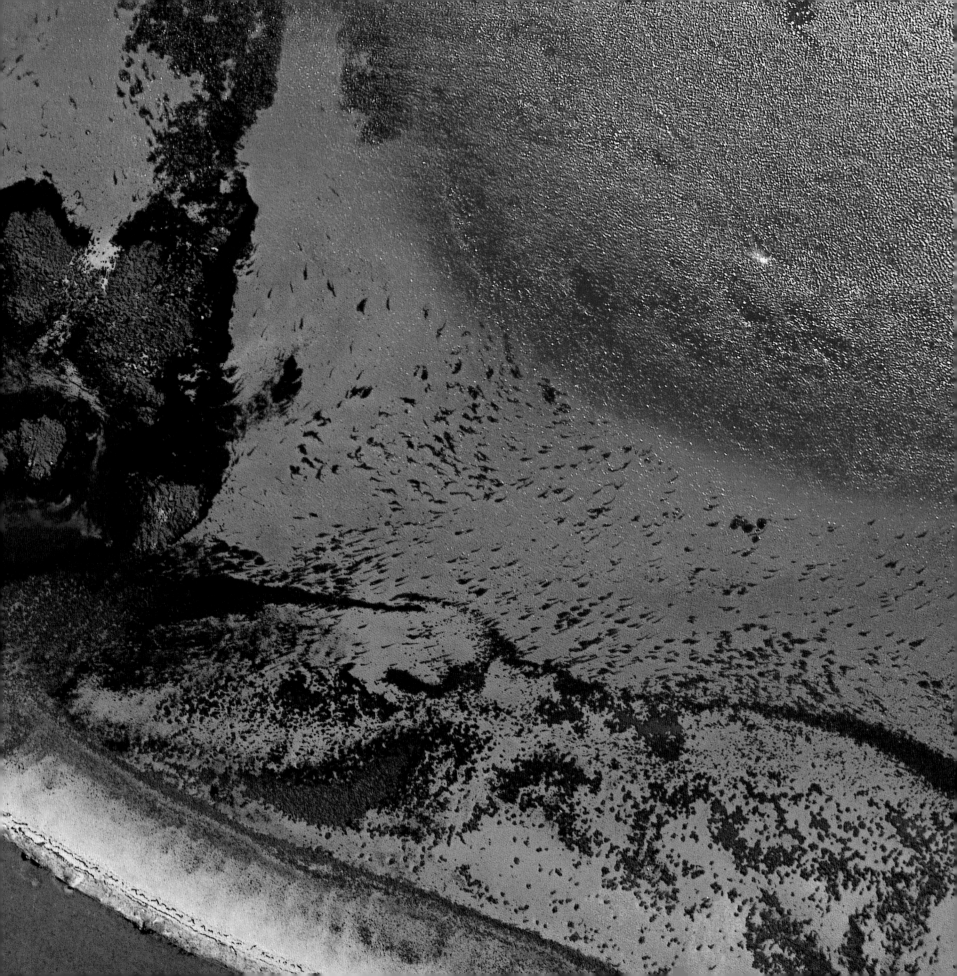

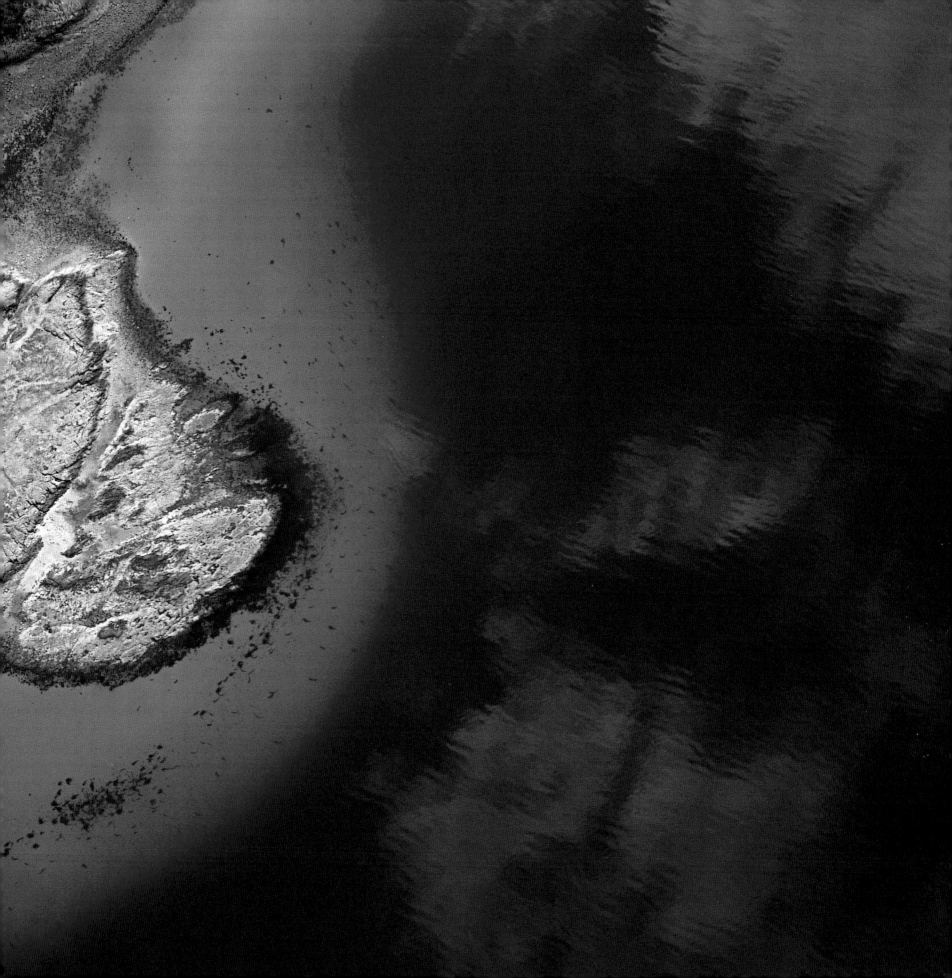

Island of Bute, Scotland

The Isle of Bute is the second biggest of the four major islands in the Clyde Estuary, the largest being Arran to the south. Bute is largely a gentle green island, without the dramatic contrasts of its larger neighbour.

Island of Bute, Scotland

The island is situated between the southern flank of the Cowal peninsula and the western and eastern banks of the River Clyde.

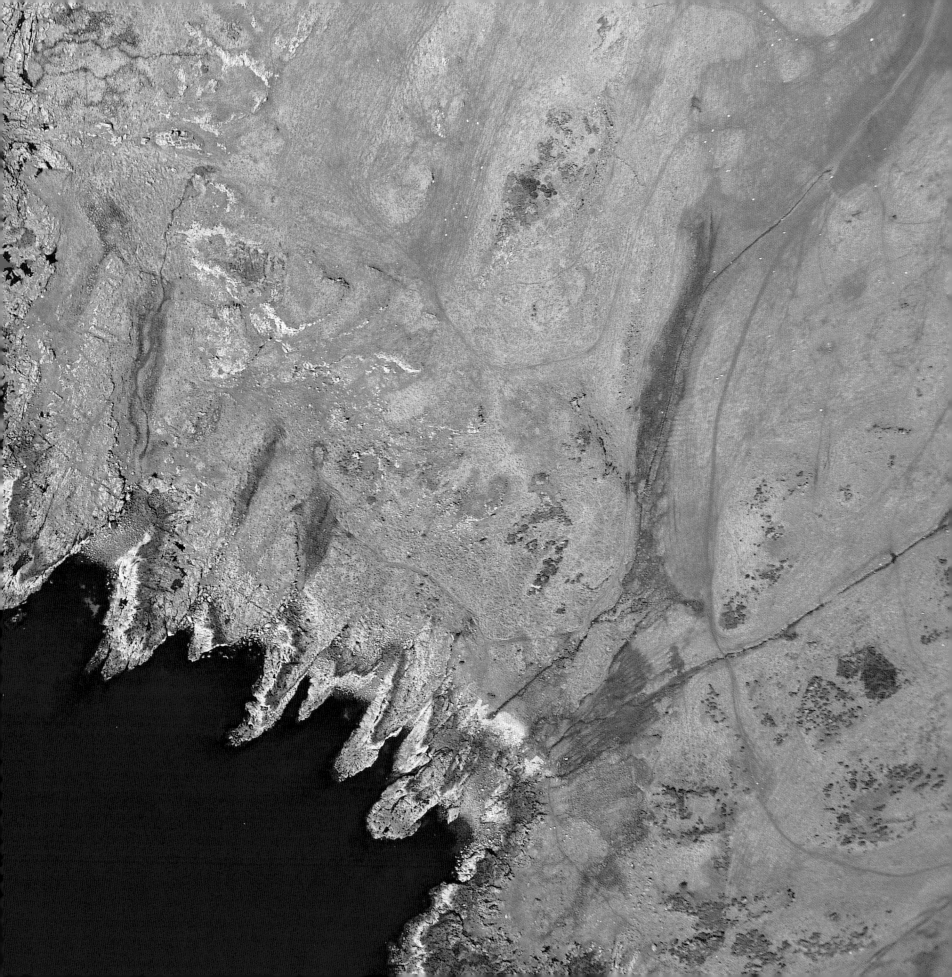

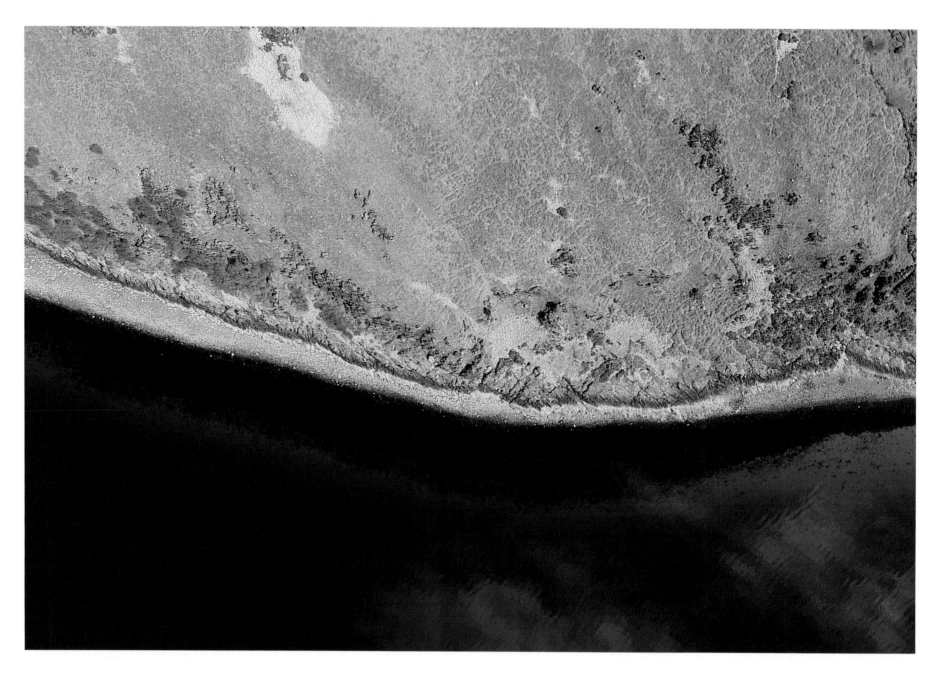

Island of Bute, Scotland

The waters surrounding Bute are fed by the Gulf Stream or Atlantic Drift, providing a very temperate climate. In fact, it is so mild that palm trees flourish on the Island.

Island of Bute, Scotland

Bute has been inhabited since at least 4000BC.
The earliest evidence is a Neolithic burial cairn
at Gleackbrae.

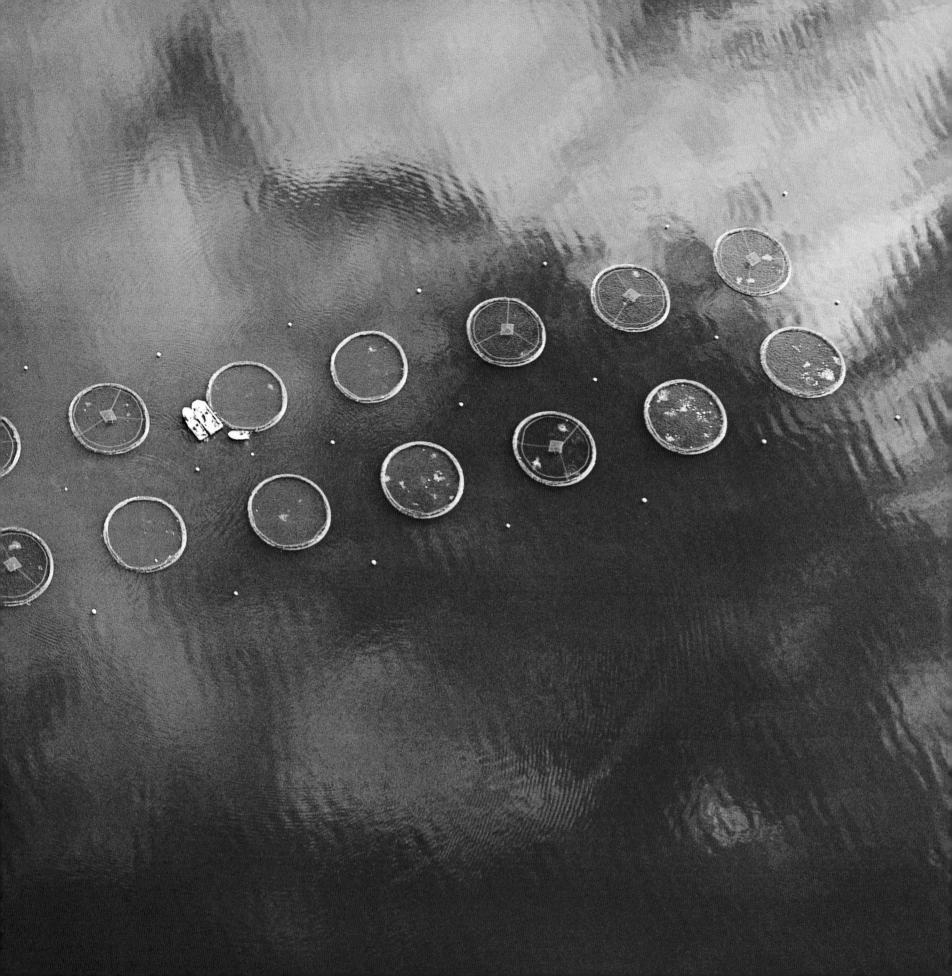

PREVIOUS PAGES
Fish Farming on the West Coast, Scotland
Looking like giant jelly fish on a route march across
the ocean, these floating cages are crowded with
thousands of young salmon. Although fish have
been farmed in many countries for hundreds of
years, it is relatively new to the UK, with the first
experiments taking place in the early 1960s.

West Coast, Scotland
The lure of a small harbour is irresistible: the
coming and going of boats, some large, some small,
some designed for work, others purely for the
pleasure of being on the water. The gentle ripples
of the calmed sea, piles of lobster pots and fishing
nets, tangles of old rope, vessels under repair and
the constant presence of seagulls searching for a
quick meal make harbours a picturesque focal point
for life on the coast.

Outer Hebrides, Scotland

Standing majestically at the north-west edge of Scotland, the island chain of the Outer Hebrides offers an incredible diversity of landscapes and habitats. Here, golden eagles can be seen, otters play and islands have romantic names such as Rum, Muck and Eigg.

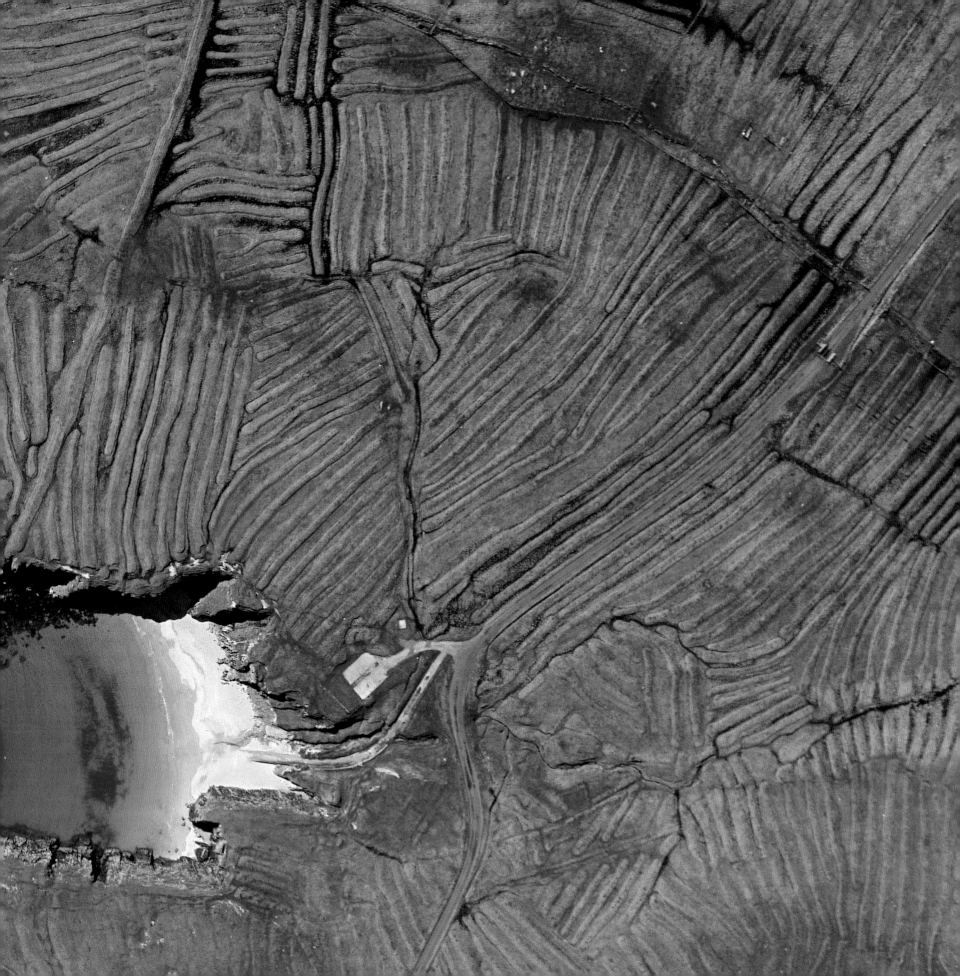

PREVIOUS PAGES
Outer Hebrides, Scotland
Along the whole Atlantic coast of the archipelago
there is a line of large shell-sand beaches, many of
which are several miles long. Clean and unspoiled,
these beaches are regularly voted among the finest
in Europe.

Outer Hebrides, Scotland
The gentle ebb and flow of the tide over sand lulls one
into feeling that the sea is a benign and gentle place,
but in its angry moments it can destroy everything in
its path. Over millennia man has learned to live with
the sea, but never managed to tame it.

Outer Hebrides, Scotland

No other known planet is as watery as Earth and
ninety-seven per cent of the water on Earth is
contained in the sea. Oceans, seas and gulfs account
for nearly three quarters of the Earth's surface. The sea
is also vital to life on our planet as minute plankton
produce most of the free oxygen we breathe.

Outer Hebrides, Scotland

Throughout the Outer Hebrides there is evidence of past civilizations. Standing stones, such as those at Callanish on Lewis (which predate the Egyptian Pyramids), or the seventh-century Celtic cross from North Rona, show how people have braved the elements on these small islands for thousands of years.

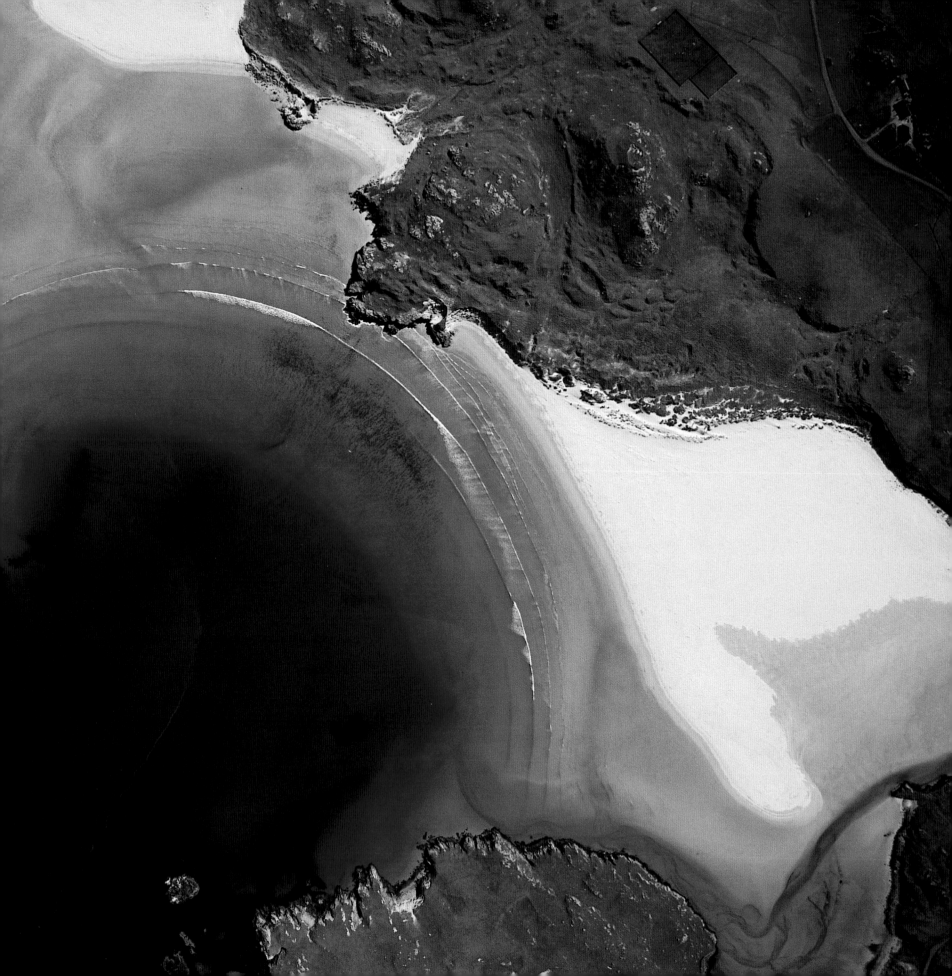

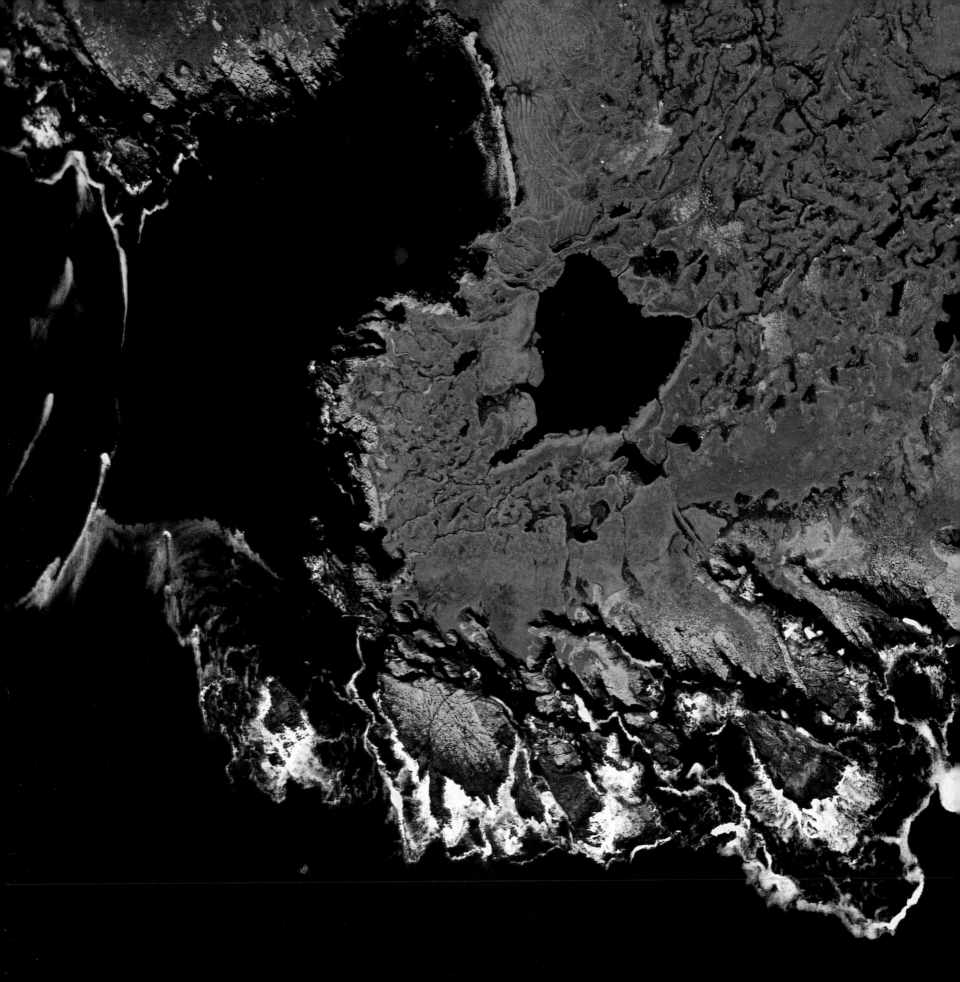

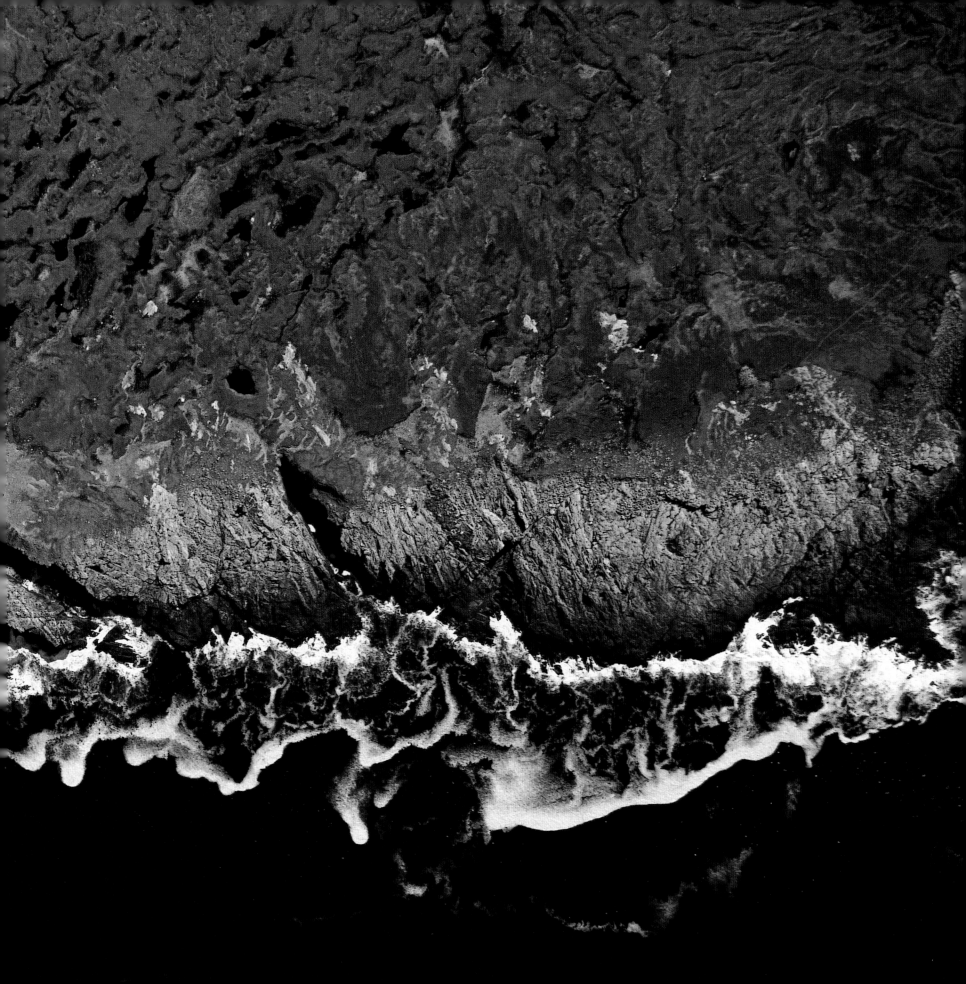

Outer Hebrides, Scotland

The west coast of these islands experiences the
full impact of the North Atlantic swells and has
the most consistent surf in Europe, making
it an essential destination for surfers.

Outer Hebrides, Scotland

The name Harris comes from the old Norse word
meaning 'high land' and the island is often
described as the 'high heart of the Hebrides'. The
east coast is a dramatic, rocky landscape, where
it is hard to imagine how people have managed to
scrape a living from the land and sea.

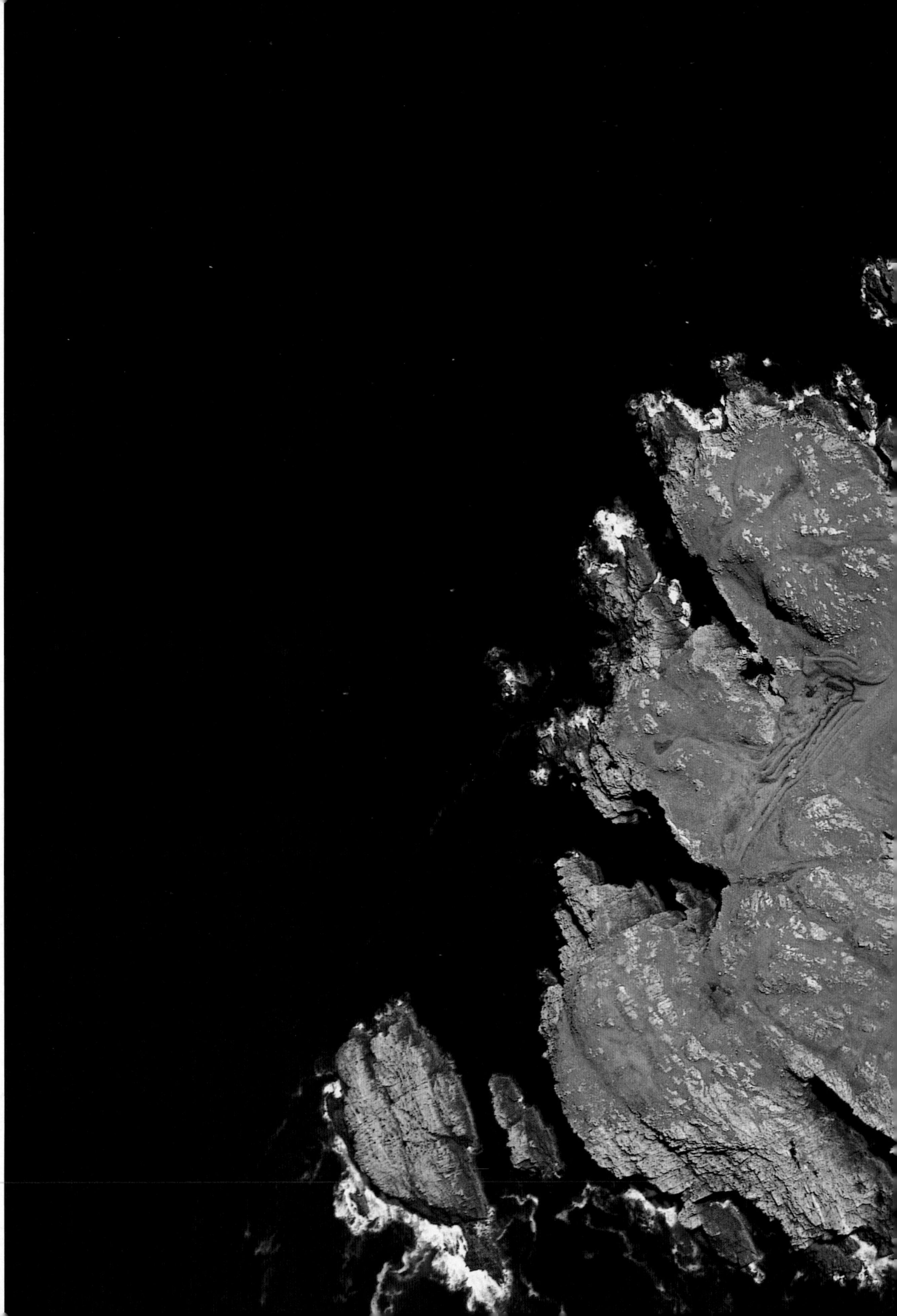

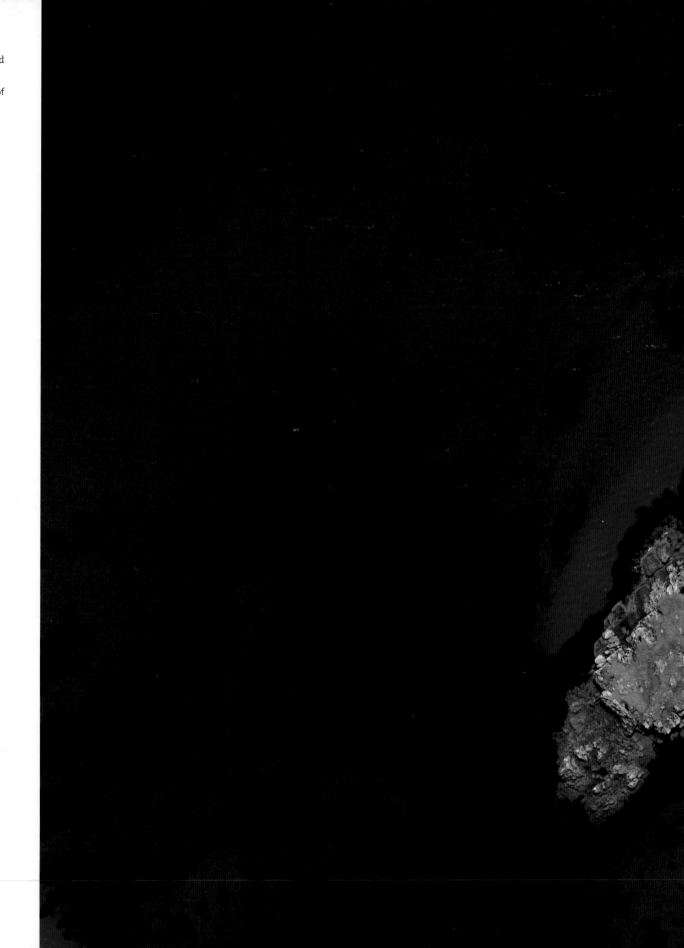

Outer Hebrides, Scotland
The peaceful uninhabited islands dotted around the Hebrides are treasure troves. Visiting these islands is a real adventure, where the pleasure of seeing beautiful landscapes and rare species is coupled with the excitement of exploring untouched and isolated locations.

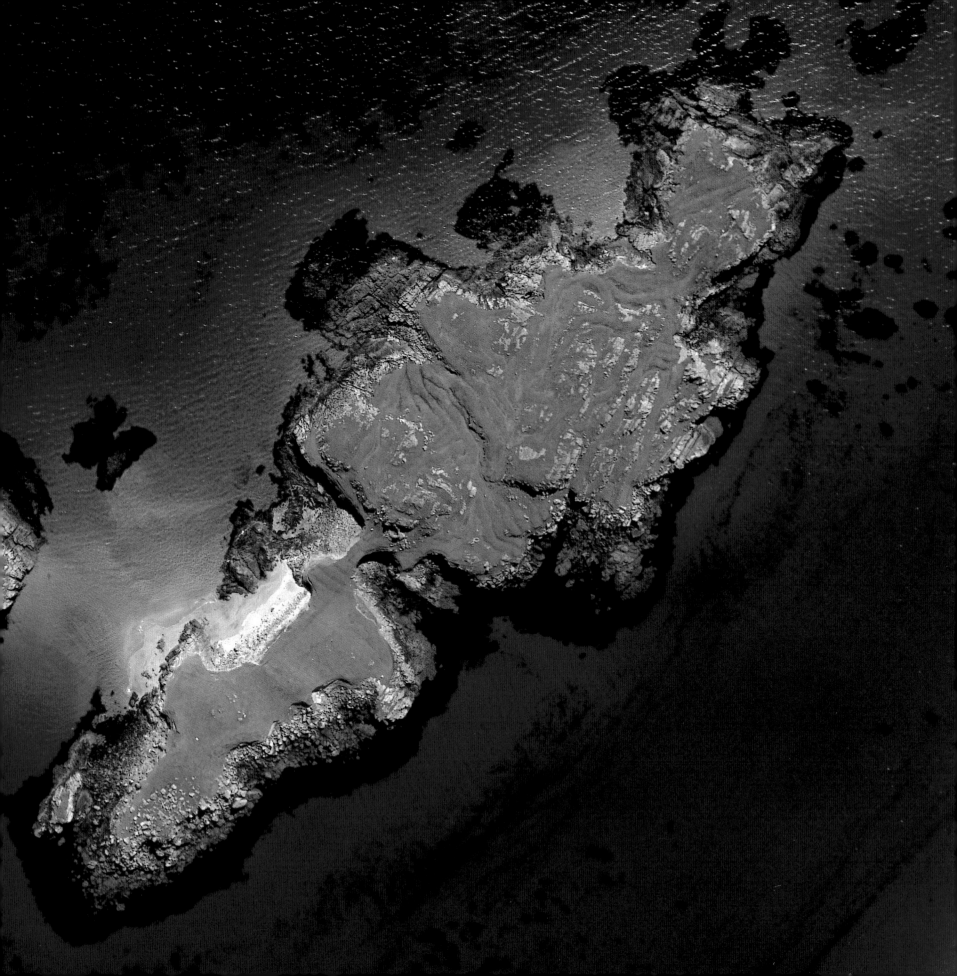

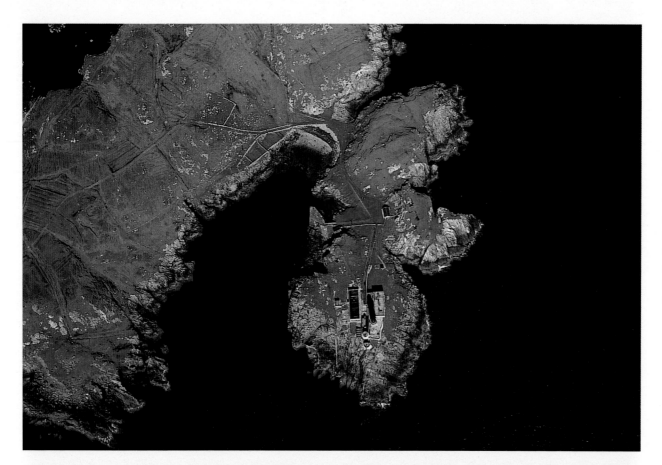

LEFT

Outer Hebrides, Scotland

East Loch Tarbert is the large sea inlet that lies between south Harris and north Harris. East Loch Tarbert and West Loch Tarbert almost separate north Harris from south Harris, which are joined by a small isthmus.

BELOW LEFT

Outer Hebrides, Scotland

Tarbert is the main port and capital village of Harris. Tarbert is a fairly common name across Scotland and, here as elsewhere, it comes from the Norse *tairbeart*, which means draw-boat. Little existed here until Tarbert was formed as a fishing settlement in about 1779. From 1840 a new pier in East Loch Tarbert was the destination of weekly mail steamers from Skye, serving the new postal district called Harris.

RIGHT
Outer Hebrides, Scotland
The severe weather patterns of the North Atlantic, coupled with a rocky coast, make the waters around the Hebrides extremely hazardous, as this shipwreck demonstrates.

BELOW RIGHT
Outer Hebrides, Scotland
The islands are full of rare and iconic species such as the puffin, golden eagle, basking shark, whale, dolphin, otter and corncrake.

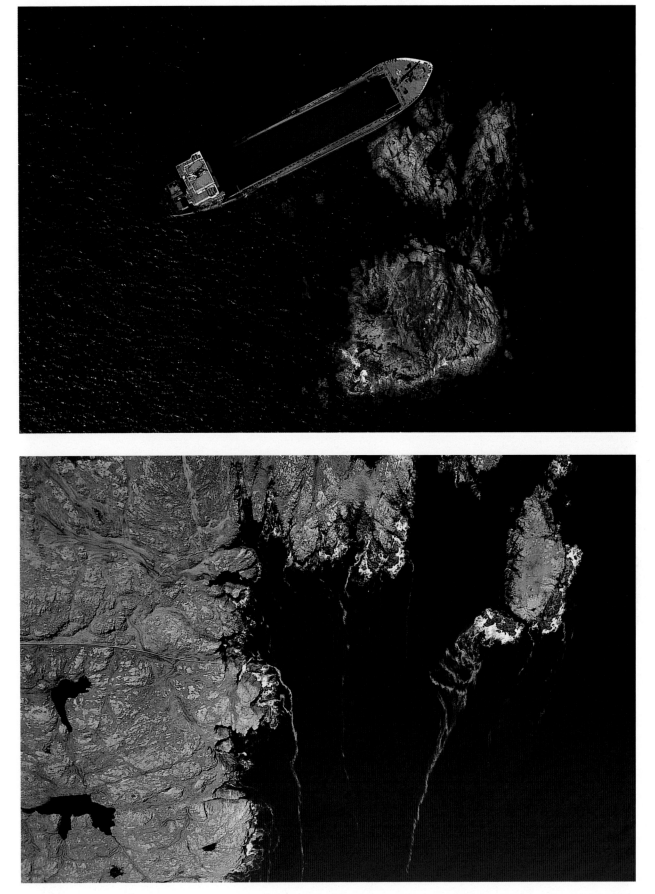

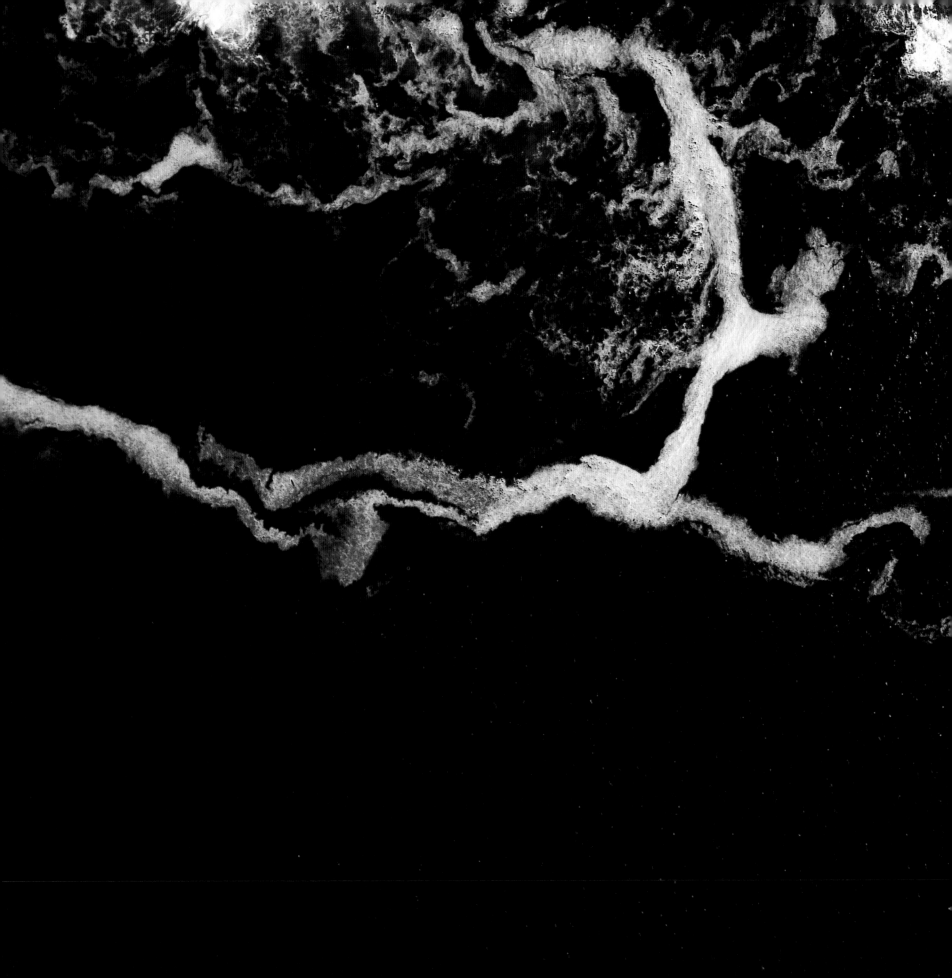

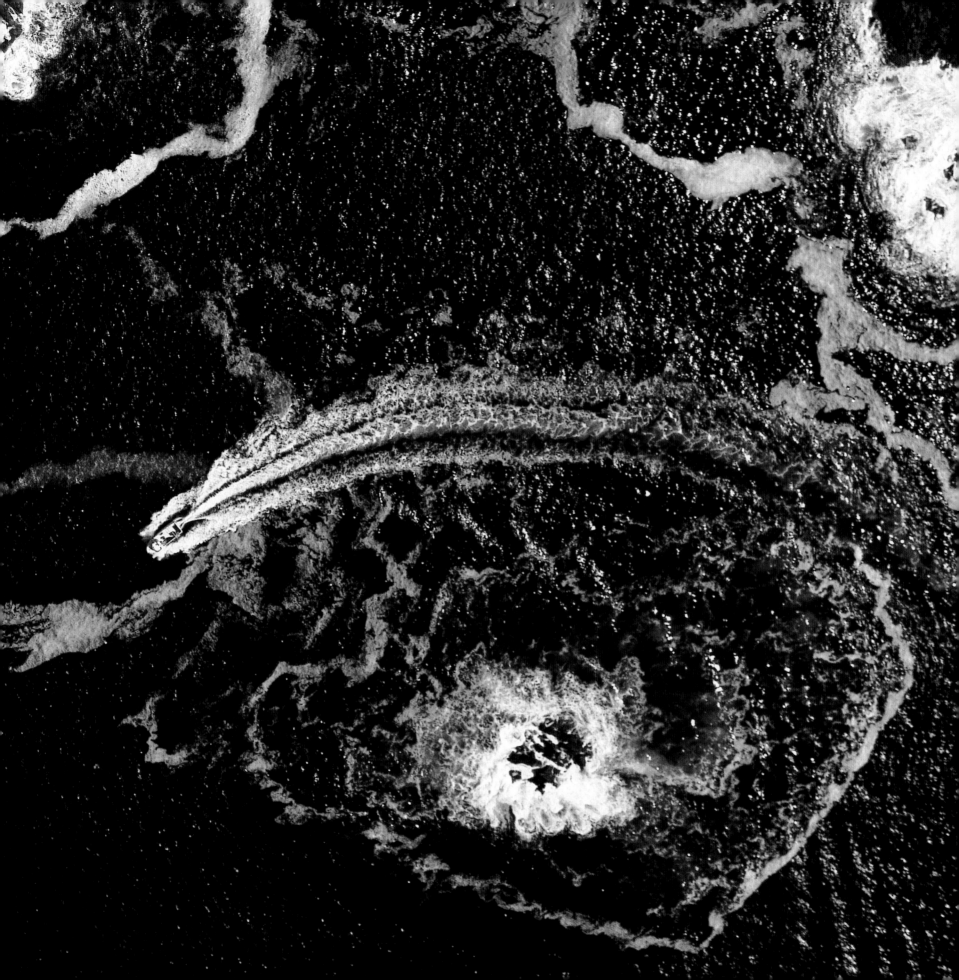

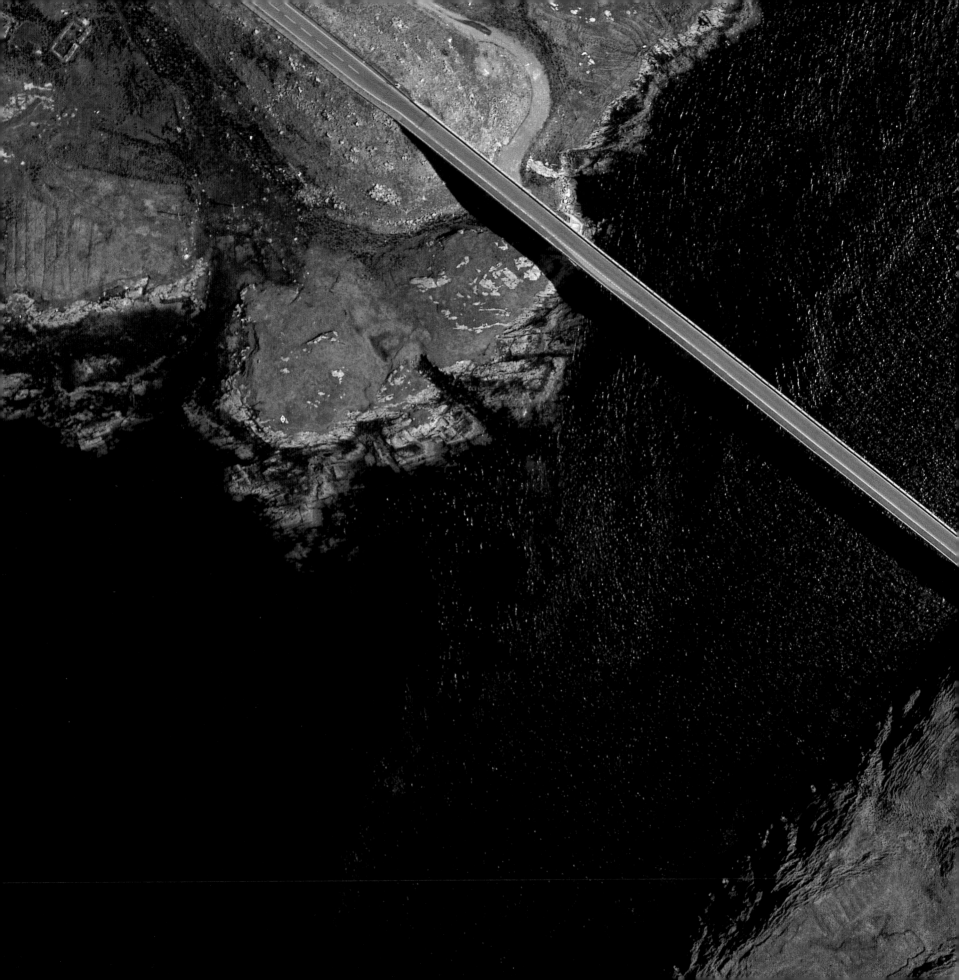

PREVIOUS PAGES
Outer Hebrides, Scotland

The sea warms and cools more slowly than land, giving the coasts of the continents cooler summers and warmer winters than inland areas. The oceans are also the birthplace of most of the storms that affect climate throughout the world.

Outer Hebrides, Scotland

The terrain of this archipelago makes travel between islands difficult without a boat, but the main islands are interconnected by a road, which winds its way around the islands, crossing between them by a series of bridges.

Outer Hebrides, Scotland
Some of the mountains on the Outer Hebrides date back seven hundred and fifty million years. Their barren slopes, like a strange and awe-inspiring lunar landscape, often boast snow-capped summits. They add to the dramatic and breathtaking scenery of this inhospitable place.

Loch Shawbost, Lewis, Scotland

The incredible machair lands and dunes alongside these beaches are brimming with flowers and wildlife such as corncrakes and otters. Long and linear, the east coast of South Uist is composed of fjordic inlets and bays. The Loch Druidibeg nature reserve is a fantastic day out on a crisp winter's day.

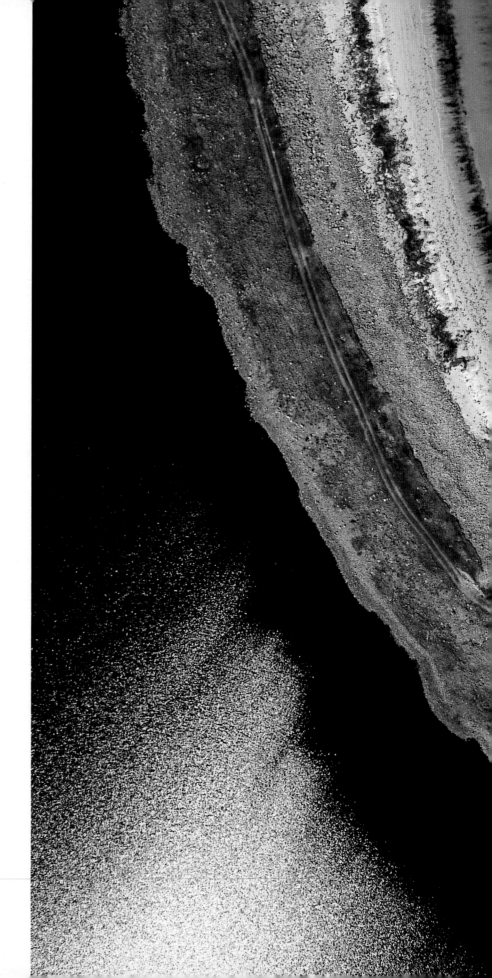

Loch Shawbost, Lewis, Scotland
What is not peat bog and water on Lewis is mostly
rock, shared by sheep and a few straggling crofts.
The crofting tradition declined throughout the
twentieth century and continues to do so, as more
attractive lifestyles beckon on the mainland.

Loch Shawbost, Lewis, Scotland
The beaches of these islands are shell-white strips of
incredible beauty, mediating between a rocky
landscape and an Atlantic of a rare seductive blue.
There is nothing but waves until you reach America.

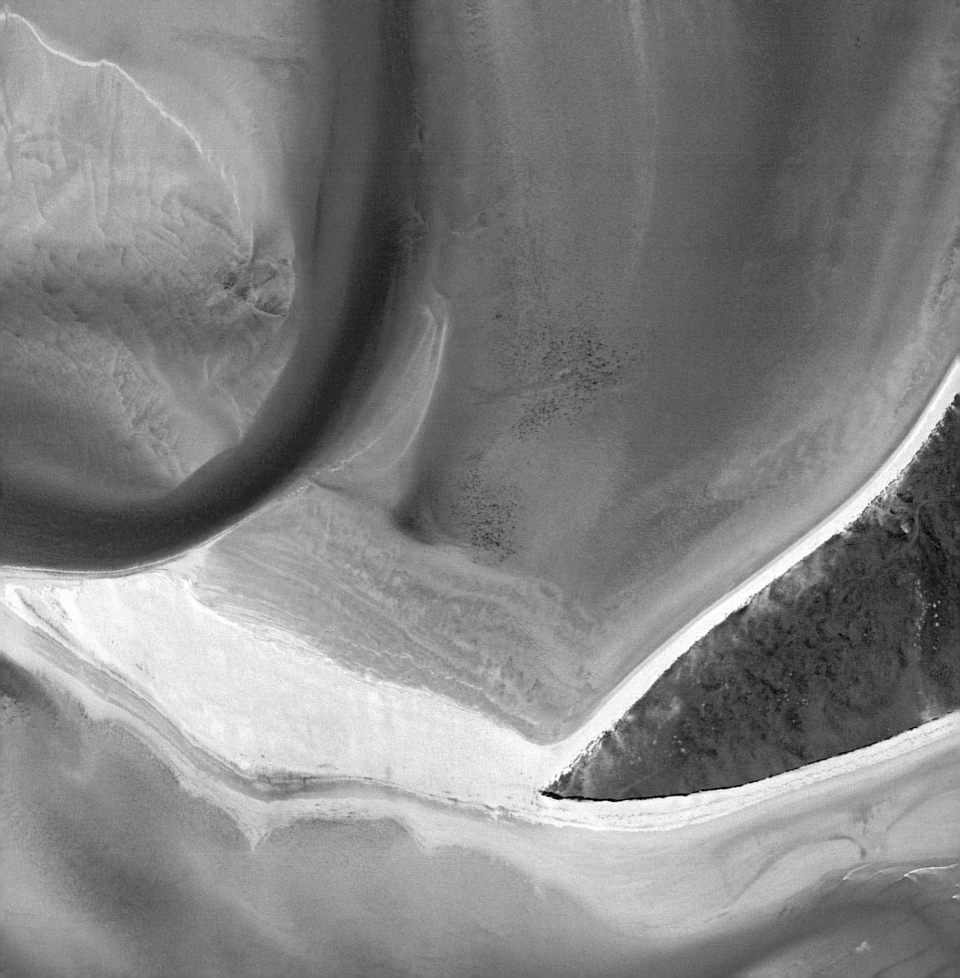

PREVIOUS PAGES

Luskentyre, Scotland

Luskentyre has miles of rippled, estuarine sand carrying nothing but the footprints of sea birds. These beaches stretch like a bolt of watered silk between the tweedy greens and browns of north Harris and the burial island of Taransay.

St Abb's Head, Scotland

Formed by an extinct volcano, St Abb's Head is the best-known landmark along the Berwickshire coast. Home to thousands of nesting seabirds, including guillemots, razorbills, shags, fulmars and puffins, the head is covered with a profusion of wild flowers in spring and summer.

Eyemouth, Scotland

In 1881 Eyemouth suffered a terrible fishing disaster when one hundred and twenty-nine men (from a population of less than three thousand) perished in a single afternoon. It was a cataclysm which rocked the little town and is remembered as 'Black Friday'. The bay at Eyemouth is virtually the only safe landing place in Berwickshire and there has been a settlement here, where the River Eye meets the sea, for many centuries.

East Coast, Scotland

Buffeted all year round by strong winds and rough
seas, this area of the British coastline has a startling
beauty and a long history of battles between
invaders and those trying to resist their conquest.
First the Vikings came to maraud and plunder,
followed in subsequent centuries by skirmishes
between the Scots and English.

East Coast, Scotland

East Lothian's spectacular coastal scenery has many
geological stories to tell. The sweeping beaches,
rocky headlands and steep cliffs are the result of a
variety of rocks that record changing environments
and conditions over one hundred and fifty million
years. The remains of volcanic eruptions, warm
tropical seas with coral reefs, and desert planes can
be found here.

Since it does not have to face the onslaught of the Atlantic and can claim very little in the way of significant upland, it is hardly surprising that Britain's eastern shoreline should be altogether gentler in most ways than its western counterpart. Nevertheless, man has ensured that the picture from the air is still a fascinating one of varied form and colour.

In England, the beaches of Northumberland lead south to the bays and cliffs of Yorkshire, famous for their elegant holiday resorts. Discreet villages on quiet creeks around the Norfolk and Suffolk coastline are a quiet prelude to the powerful patterns created by the marshes and mudflats of Essex and the Thames Estuary.

The Humber Bridge, East Coast

The Humber is one of the major estuaries in the UK, with a deepwater channel 22 miles long from the open sea at Spurn Head to the port of Kingston-upon-Hull.

Until 1981, this was the last major unbridged estuary in Britain, causing a barrier to trade and development between the two banks. In that year the graceful Humber Bridge was opened to traffic for the first time, effectively linking two previously remote and insular areas of England and saving many millions of vehicle miles per year and many valuable hours of drivers' and passengers' time. For seventeen years, it held the record as the longest single-span suspension bridge in the world.

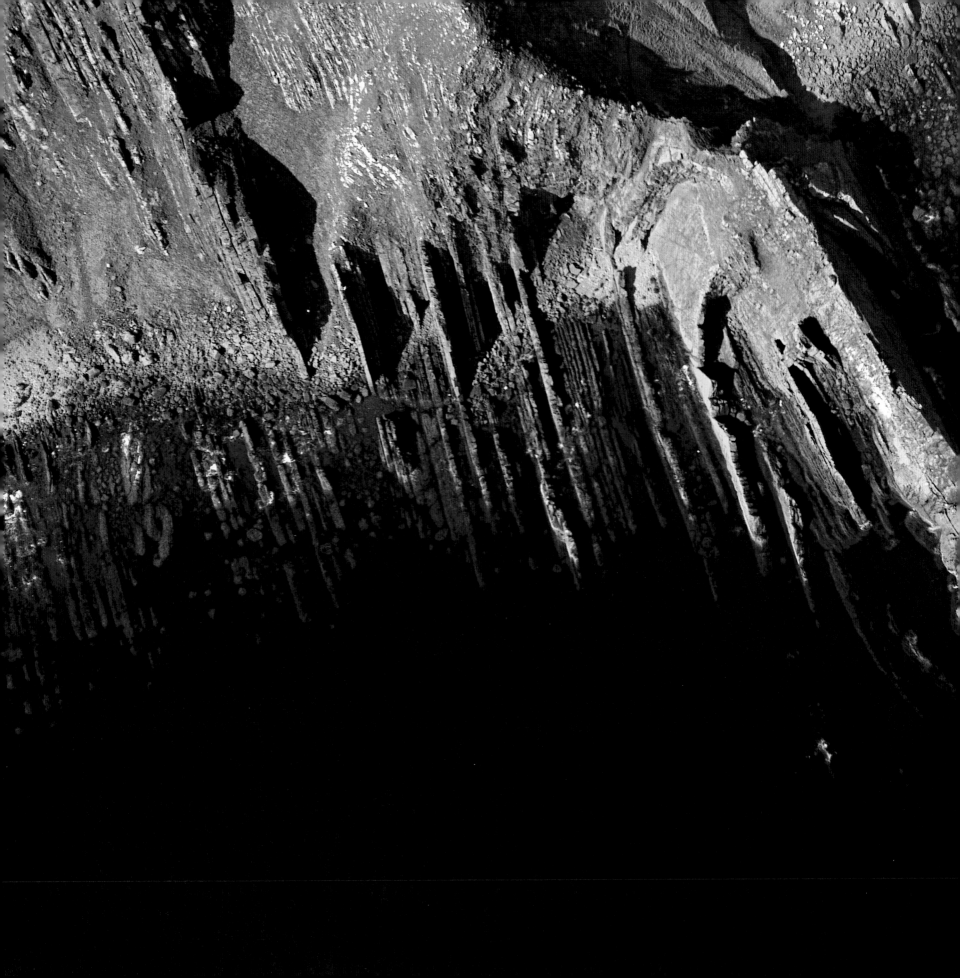

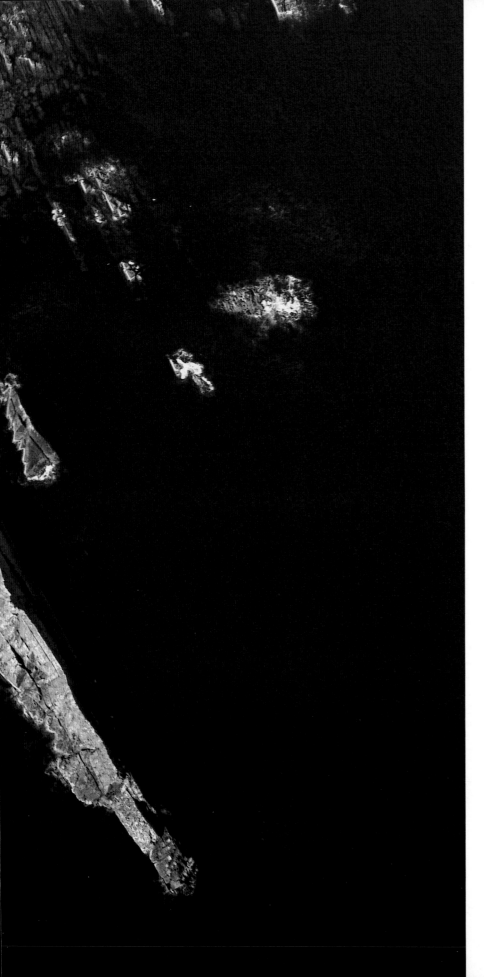

Berwick-upon-Tweed, Northumberland
Characterized by folded sedimentary rocks, the rugged scenery of the Berwickshire coast includes cliffs rising one hundred metres above the water and the spectacle of thousands of nesting seabirds between April and July. Geological and archaeological features demonstrate sedimentation, volcanic activity and human history – from Iron Age settlements to a medieval monastery and nineteenth-century lighthouse.

NEXT PAGES
Lindisfarne, Northumberland
In the tidal, estuary-like mudflats of Budle Bay is Holy Island, still often known by its more ancient name of Lindisfarne. Life on this island is controlled by the tide. The only access to it is across a meandering causeway, which is completely submerged at high tide.

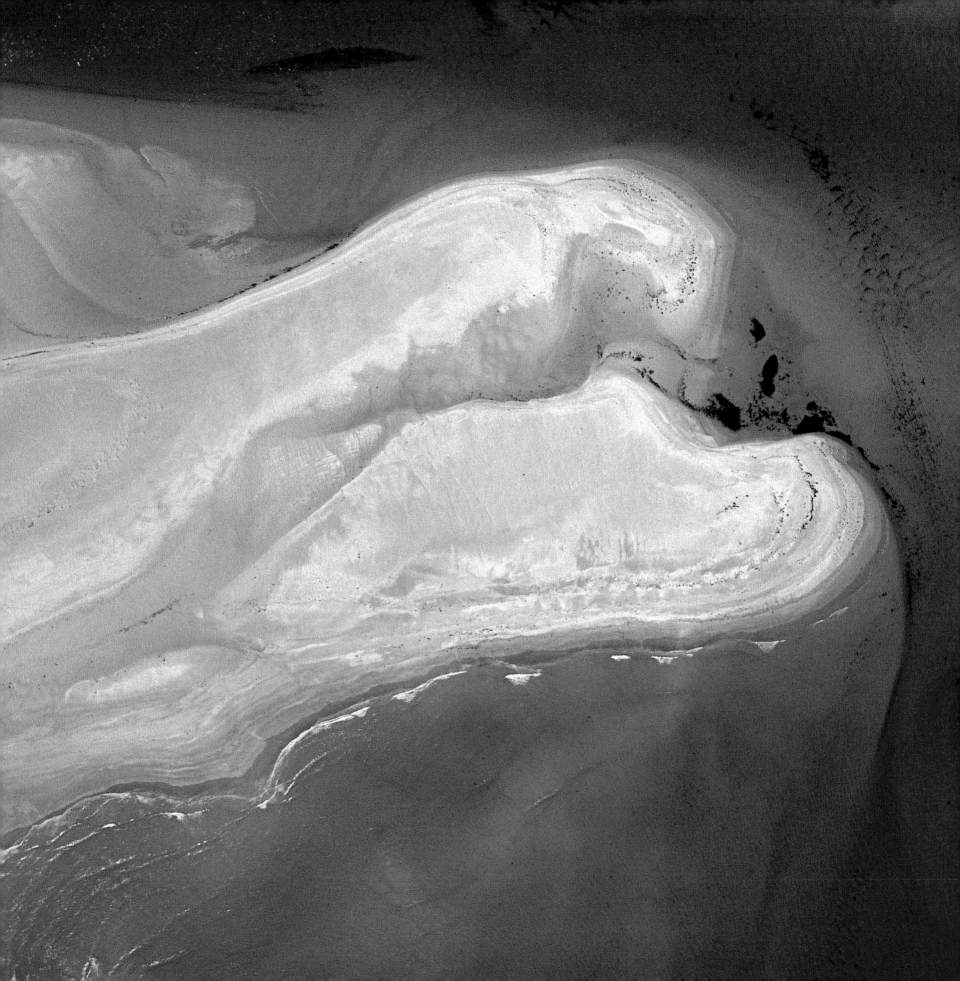

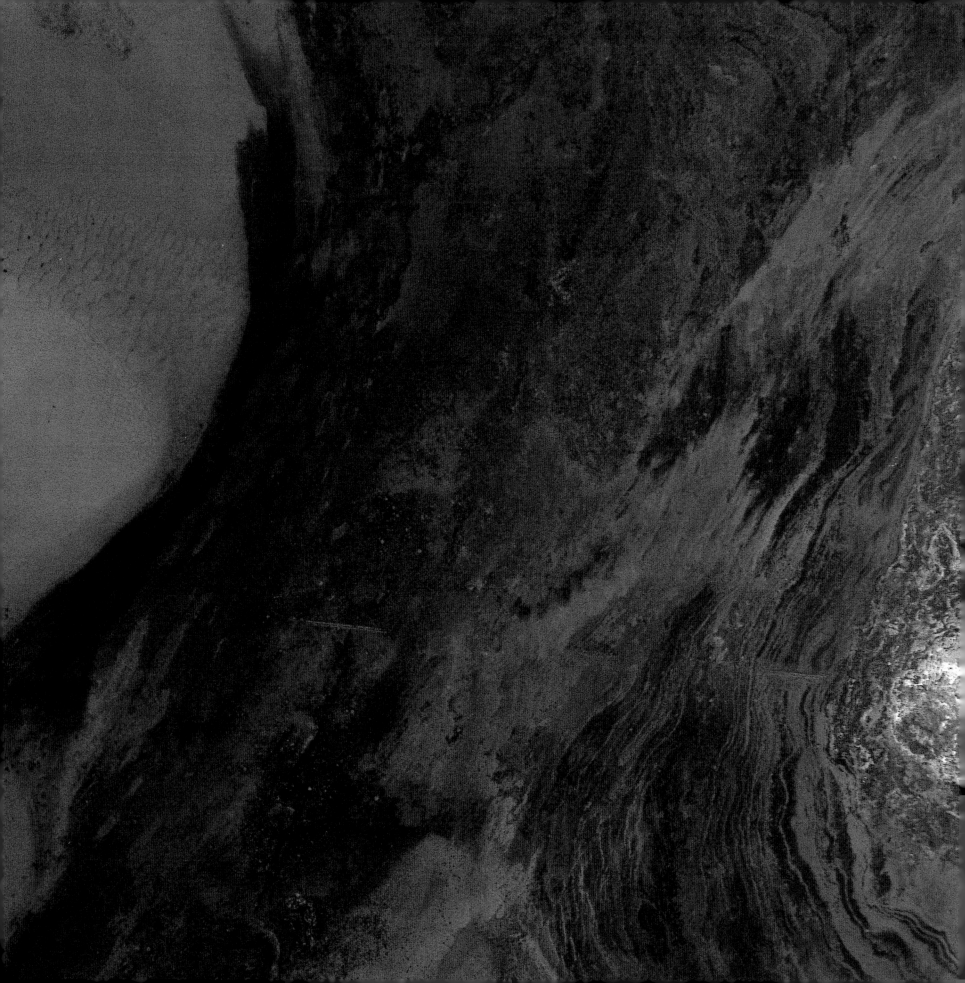

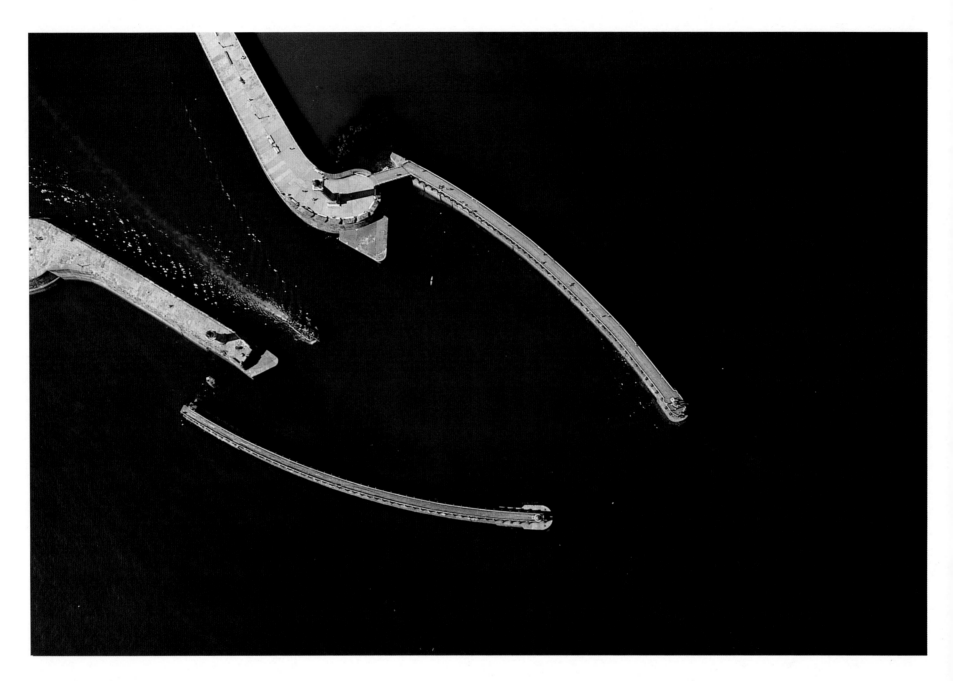

Whitby, North Yorkshire

From this harbour sailed the three ships –
Endeavour, Adventure and Revolution – on which
Captain Cook carried out his great voyages of
exploration around the world. All three were built
here in Whitby, which has an illustrious maritime
history dating back to Roman times. Whitby
provides the only natural harbour between the
Tees and the Humber and has a long history as
a whaling port.

Whitby, North Yorkshire

Surrounded on three sides by the North Yorkshire
Moors and on the fourth side by the North Sea,
Whitby is a small picturesque fishing town famous
for its abbey high in the cliffs and its associations
with Dracula. The quaint, cobbled streets, set
around the busy harbour, and the 199 steps which
lead to the parish church of St Mary were well
known to Bram Stoker, who used this setting for his
famous Gothic novel.

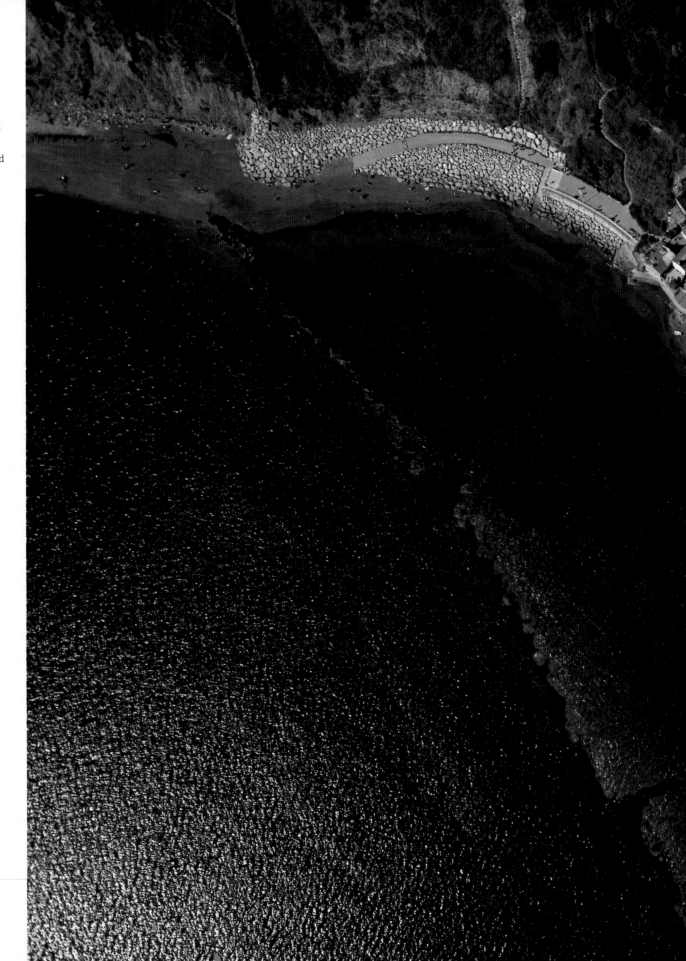

Robin Hood's Bay, North Yorkshire

Legend has it that Robin Hood came to Whitby to help the abbot repel Danish invaders, giving his name to the bay in which he fought them. The cliffs around this bay are some of the highest on the east coast of Britain and have long been mined for their alum, which was used in the woollen industry as a mordant for dyes. Twisting streets and tiny russet-tiled fishermen's cottages characterize the pretty fishing village that is known locally as 'Bay Town'.

Scarborough, North Yorkshire

This town claims to be the home of the seaside holiday. In the mid-seventeenth century Dr Robert Wittie advocated the use of seawater and advised gout sufferers to bathe at Scarborough. It so happened that from the side of a cliff overlooking the beach, there flowed a mineral spring which had attracted patients to take the waters since 1627. Because it mixed with seawater, this spring had a salty taste and was considered to have purgative virtues that were extremely beneficial to those seeking a cure. Many going to Scarborough to take the cure combined drinking this water with excursions along the beach and strand at low tide. So began the British tradition of spending holidays at the seaside.

Filey Brigg, North Yorkshire

Filey Brigg is a finger of limestone that juts almost half a mile out to sea. The Brigg and Flamborough Head to the south form natural breakwaters for Filey Bay. The cliffs here are not as high as those further up towards Robin Hood's Bay, but orchids are frequently found growing here.

Flamborough Head, East Yorkshire

Like a great nose, Flamborough Head is where
the Yorkshire Wolds meet the sea and where the
coast of the East Riding of Yorkshire meets North
Yorkshire. In the Iron Age headland was the site of a
great fort which was protected on the land side by
an ancient earthwork. Later, an Anglo-Saxon called
Flein settled in the area and the name Flamborough
means 'Flein's fort'.

This is one of the most dramatic and
treacherous areas of the east coast, with jagged
crags and coves gouged out of the chalk by the sea
and dangerous currents for boats to navigate.
A lighthouse was built here in 1806 to warn ships
of the impending danger.

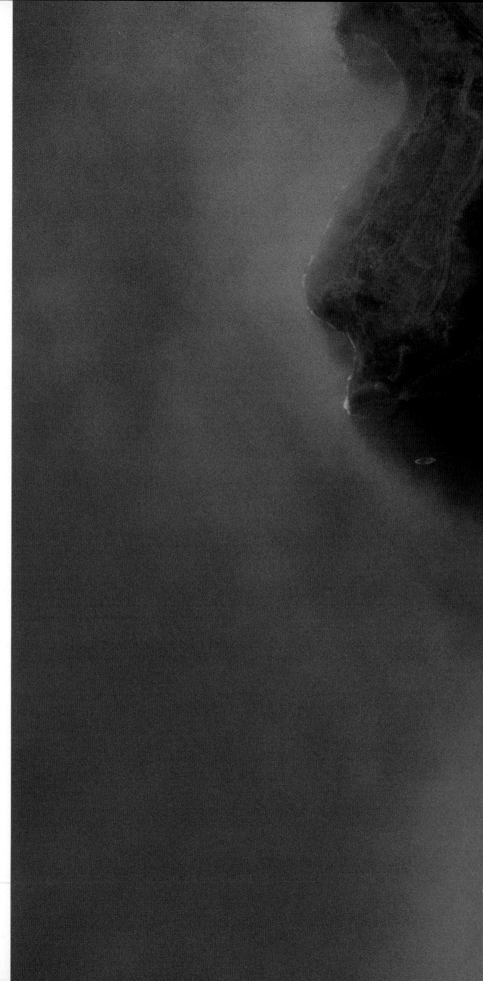

Flamborough Head, East Yorkshire
The coastline to the south of Bridlington and
Flamborough Head is said to be the fastest-
eroding coastline in Europe and is estimated to
be disappearing at around two metres per year.
The sea relentlessly eats away at the red, muddy
cliffs, gradually reclaiming for its own the flat
farmland of Holderness.

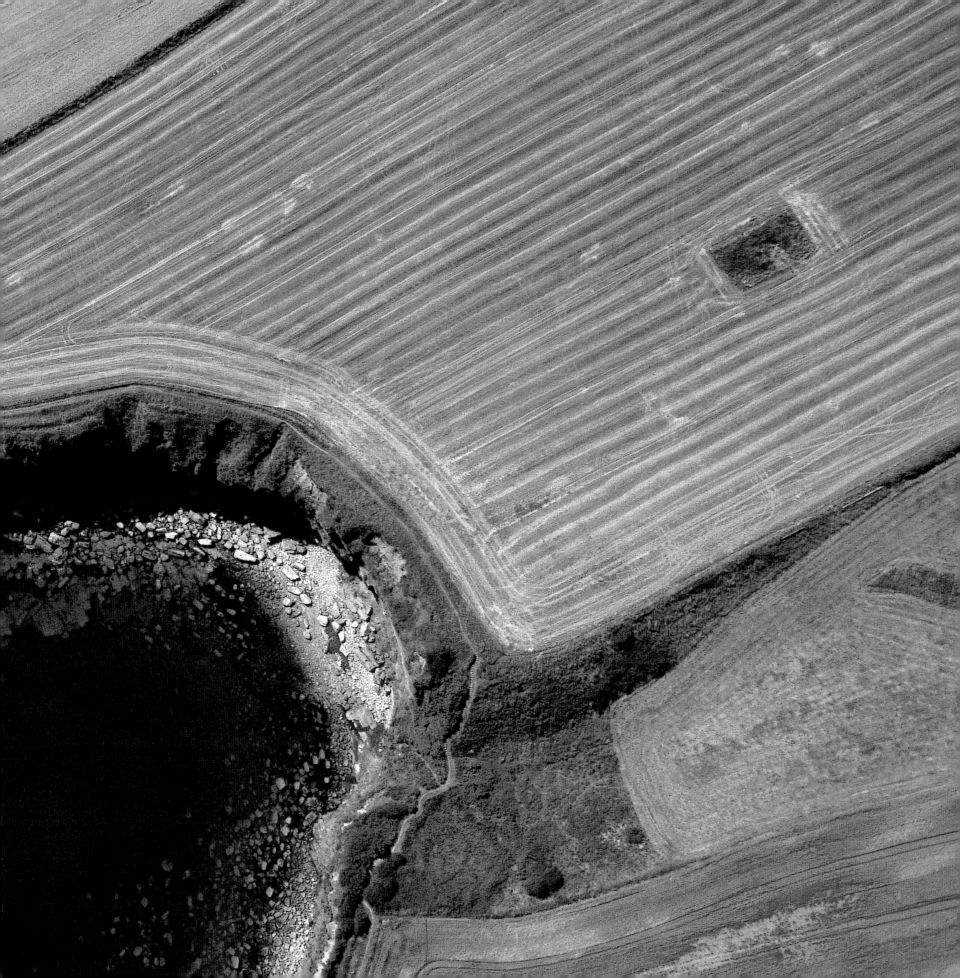

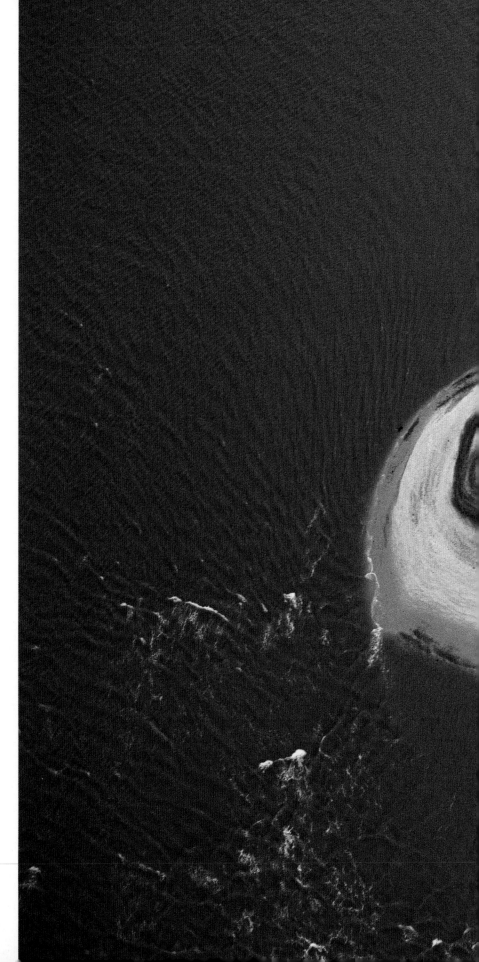

PREVIOUS PAGES

North Yorkshire Coast

Wild flowers and insects, acres of farmland, rock pools filled with sea creatures, fantastic beaches and stunning views all characterize the spectacular North Yorkshire coast. Traversed by the Cleveland Way footpath, this is a popular area with holidaymakers and walkers alike.

Blakeney Point, Norfolk

In 1912 the ever-changing landscape of shingle, sand dunes and salt marsh at Blakeney Point in north Norfolk was purchased and presented to the National Trust by anonymous individuals. It was given on the condition that its ecological balance of fauna and flora be preserved. Today this dune system, a national nature reserve, provides for nesting colonies of terns, oystercatchers, ringed plovers, avocet and many migrant birds. A large colony of grey and common seals and a wide range of shingle and salt marsh plants draw visitors to the creeks and mudflats of this evocative place.

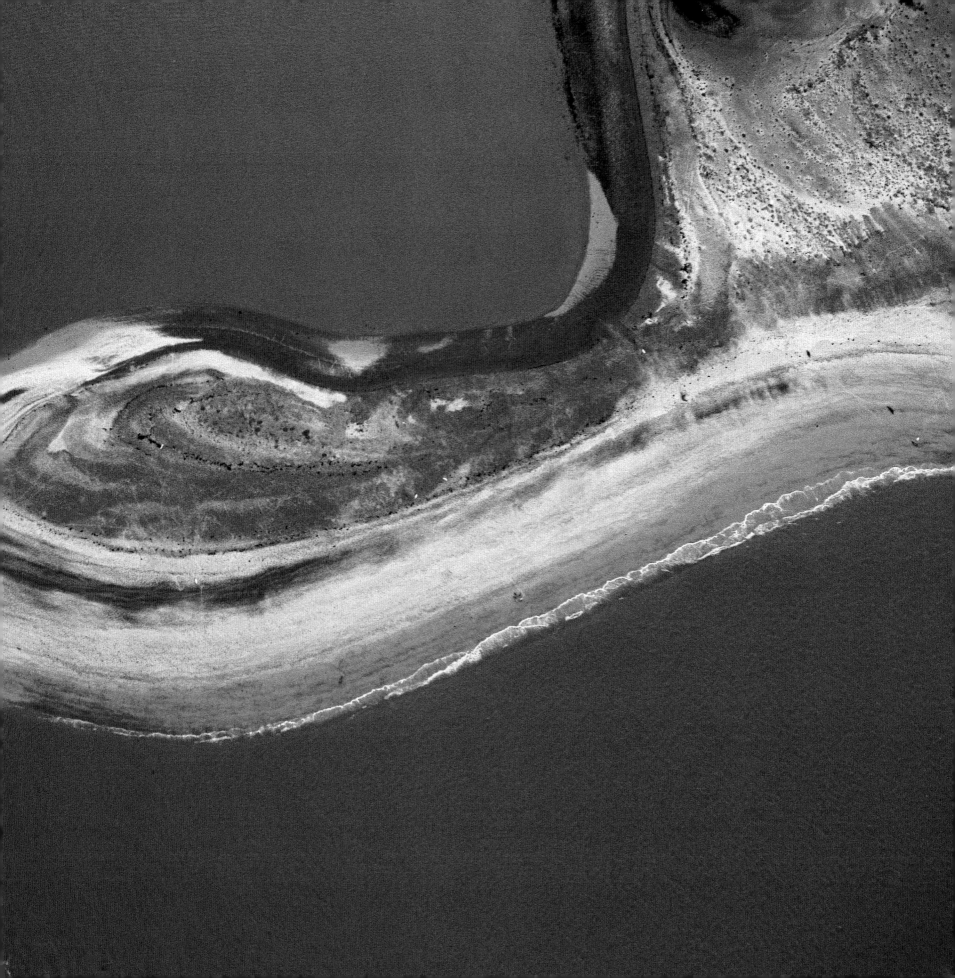

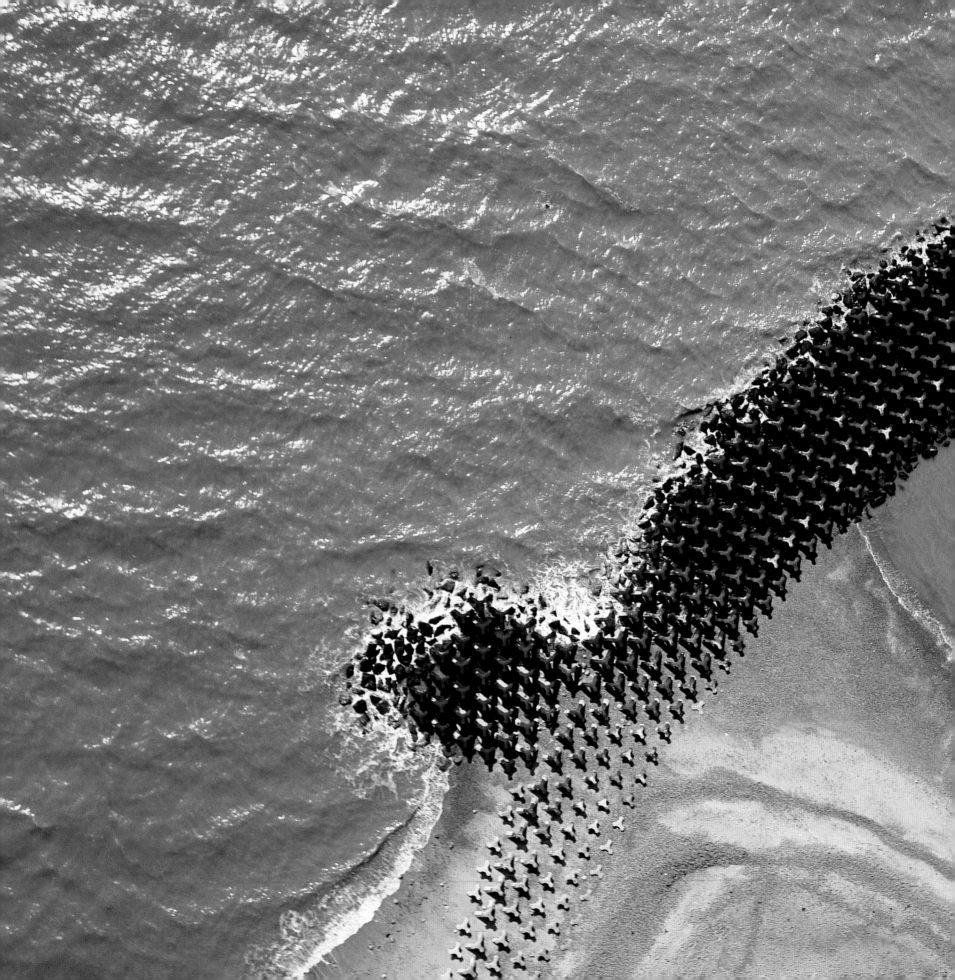

Sea Defences, Suffolk

Before Victorian engineers came on the scene, people living near the coast recognized that the shoreline needed room to adjust, particularly during winter storms. In the nineteenth century this relationship changed dramatically, mainly because civil engineers became determined to 'defend' the land against what they saw as 'attack' by the sea. Since that time, many sea walls and other protective structures such as groynes have been built.

Sea Defences, Suffolk
Building walls of sand and trying to keep back
incoming tide has long been a favourite beach
activity for youngsters. However, the coast is a
dynamic, ever-changing landscape and although
man has tried in the past to halt the sea's relentless
gnawing at his territory, all attempts have proved
futile gestures. Many have made the situation worse
rather than better.

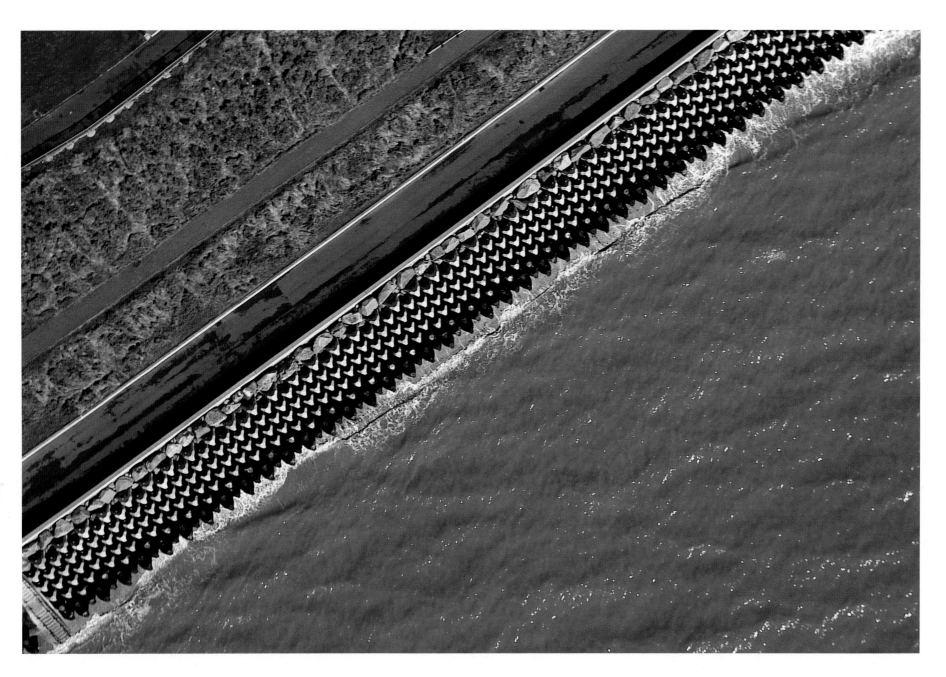

Sea Defences, Suffolk

Rather than continuing to battle with the sea,
the concept of retreating inland from the existing
line of flood defence or coast protection is now
acknowledged to be the best way forward. Whilst
inappropriate for urban areas, high-grade
agricultural land, historic or archaeological features,
elsewhere this so-called 'managed realignment'
offers a valuable opportunity for the regeneration of
coastal habitats and real ecological gains.

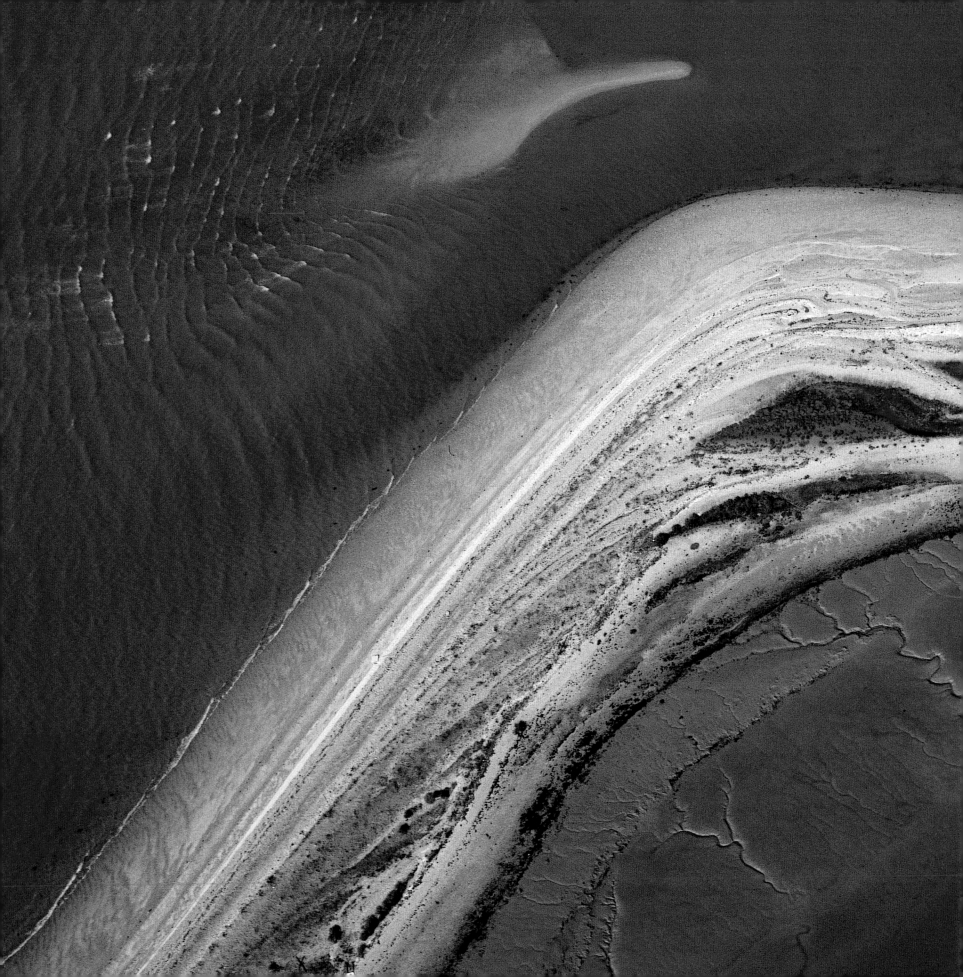

PREVIOUS PAGES

Felixstowe, Suffolk

For a century Felixstowe has been a popular, peaceful resort for family holidays, boasting record hours of sunshine, one of the lowest rainfall levels in the country and an unspoilt Victorian promenade. But there is another side to this town: the Port of Felixstowe is Britain's busiest container port, a bustling and vibrant industrial complex working round the clock, every day except Christmas Day. Felixstowe welcomed its first ship, a coal-carrying steamer, in 1886, but it was not until the 1950s that the vision of the port's founder, George Tomline, to make this one of the world's major ports, began to be realized. Today the port handles two million standard-sized containers a year – nearly half the UK's container cargo.

The Naze, Essex

The Naze derives from the Old English *naes*, meaning 'nose', and stretches 3 miles northwards from Walton-on-the-Naze. At the northern end of the Naze is Hamford Water, a large, shallow estuarine basin of tidal creeks, islands, intertidal mud and sandflats and salt marsh.

197

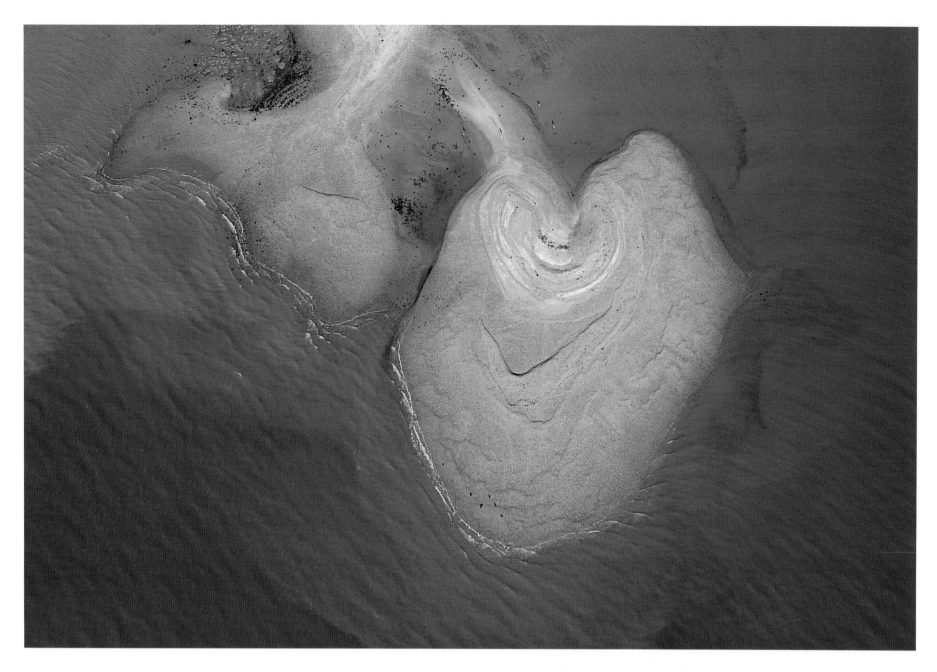

The Naze, Essex

The rich invertebrate fauna and sheltered nature
of parts of the Naze make it an internationally
important site for overwintering waders, as well
as for breeding terns in summer. These backwaters
were the setting for Arthur Ransome's book *Secret
Water*, one of the *Swallows and Amazons* series.

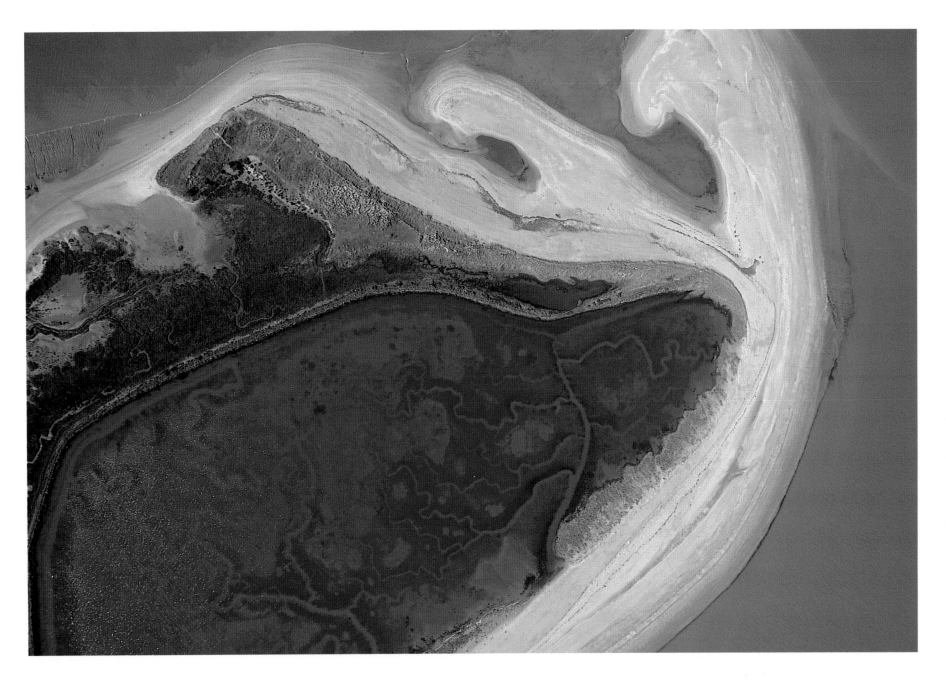

The Naze, Essex

The Naze is also of geological interest. The red crag deposits which make up the sea cliffs are quite young in geological terms, being between one and two million years old. These soft sandy deposits are the oldest Pleistocene crag deposits in Europe, but are unstable and prone to frequent collapses.

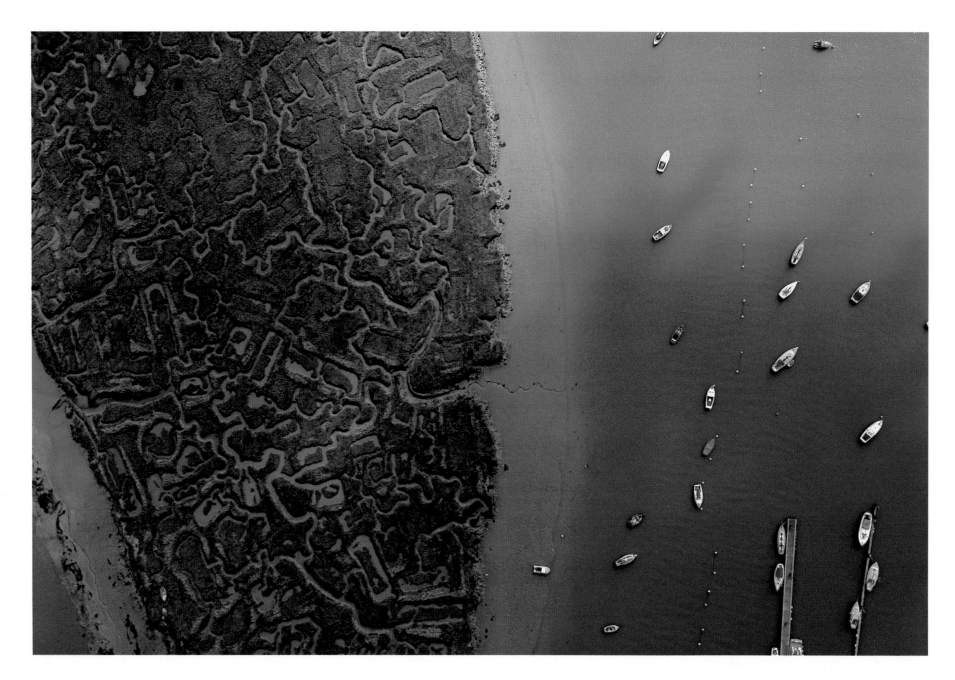

PREVIOUS PAGES
The Naze, Essex

Rising to 20 metres in height, the cliffs of the Naze
are rich in fossils and unique to the Essex coastline.
The dense scrub of hawthorn, gorse and brambles
provides cover for numerous animal species and
acts as an important landfall for migrating birds.
In summer the cliffs provide nesting sites for
sand martins.

The Blackwater Estuary, Essex

The Blackwater Estuary can be a lonely place; each
farm has its own sea wall, saltings and mudflats.
Over the past few years, an experiment has been
going on here to see what would happen if the sea
wall was removed and the sea allowed to encroach
on to agricultural land, re-claiming it as salt marsh.
It produced quick results in terms of salt-marsh
vegetation regeneration and its creation has not
only extended this type of habitat, but is also acting
as a sea defence by absorbing the wave energy.

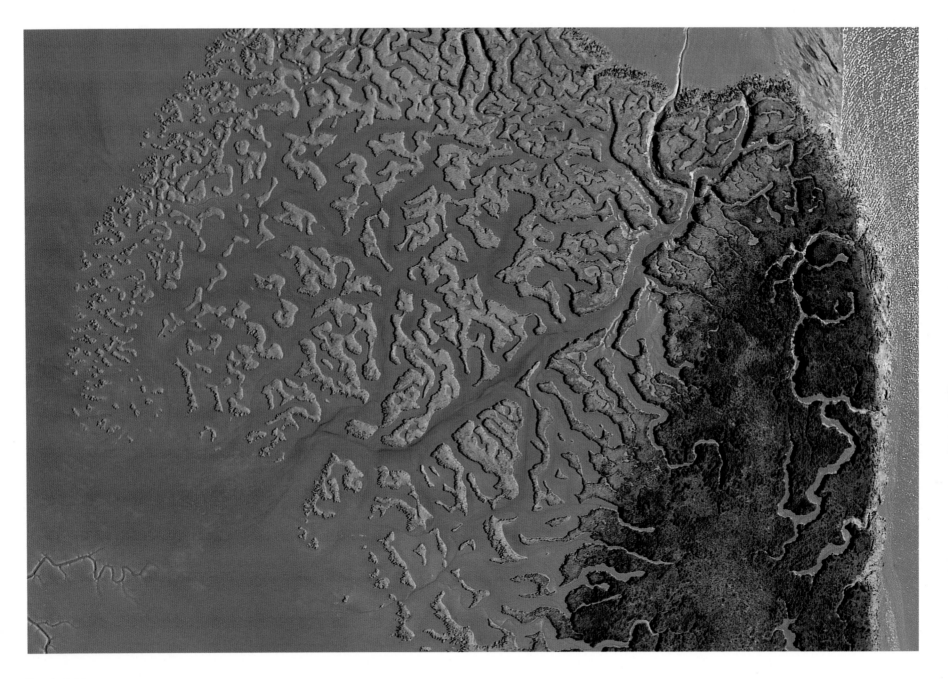

Dengie Flat, Essex

Situated on the peninsula between the estuaries of the rivers Blackwater and Crouch, the flat is a vast expanse of saltings and mudflats, named after the tiny and remote Essex village of Dengie. The whole area is designated as a Site of Special Scientific Interest for the huge flocks of Brent geese, teal and shelducks that spend the winter here.

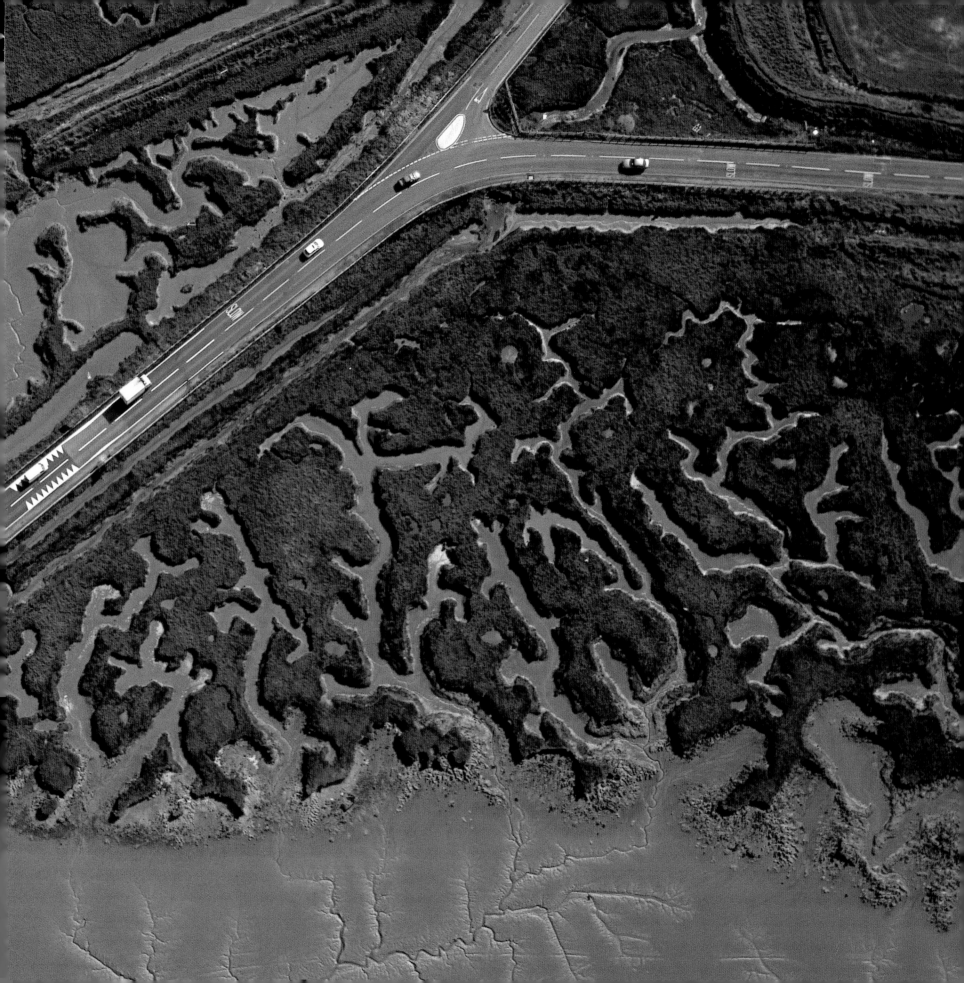

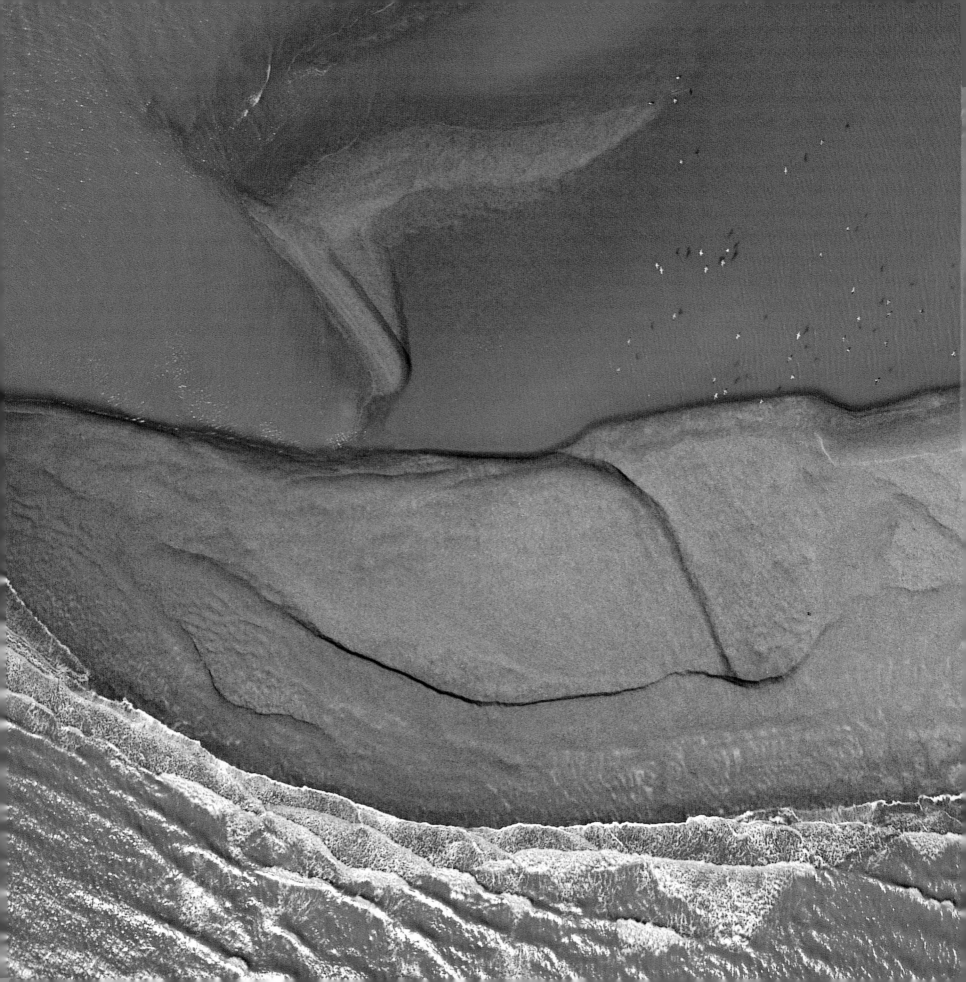

Mersea Island, Essex

Between the estuaries of the rivers Colne and Blackwater on the Essex coast lies Mersea Island, which is the most easterly inhabited island in the UK. The island is connected to the mainland by a causeway called 'The Strood', which traverses some of the most important tidal mudscapes on the east coast. These mudflats represent some of the most productive habitats we possess in this country, with the daily tidal rhythm governing the lives of all the creatures that live on or in the mud.

Blackwater Estuary, Essex

Typically every square metre of mud or sand, like this one on the Essex coast, contains hundreds of thousands of invertebrate creatures such as hydrobia (a tiny snail), ragworms and bivalves, which means a huge amount of food is available for migrant and wintering waterfowl, who take advantage of the feeding opportunities in this highly productive habitat.

Acknowledgments

Special thanks must go to all the helicopter pilots I have flown with on this project for their aerobatic skills. In particular, I would like to thank the Coastguard and Maritime Agency for their help, hospitality and cooperation. I would also like to thank Barry Robinson and Jane Ryan of the Royal Mail who initially inspired the work.

The captions in this book were written by independent consultant Richard Offen, who managed the National Trust's Neptune Coastline Campaign between 1992 and 2003.

First published in the United Kingdom in 2004 by Thames & Hudson Ltd, 181A High Holborn, London WC1V 7QX

www.thamesandhudson.com

British Library Cataloguing-in-Publication Data
A catalogue record for this book is available from the British Library

ISBN 0-500-54284-8

Printed and bound in Italy by Graphicom srl